Navigating beyond COVID-19

RECOVERY IN THE MENA REGION

Please cite this publication as:
OECD (2022), *Navigating beyond COVID-19: Recovery in the MENA Region*, OECD Publishing, Paris, https://doi.org/10.1787/48300c64-en.

ISBN 978-92-64-58975-9 (print)
ISBN 978-92-64-68194-1 (pdf)
ISBN 978-92-64-46033-1 (HTML)
ISBN 978-92-64-57965-1 (epub)

Revised version, October 2022
Details of revisions available at: https://www.oecd.org/about/publishing/Corrigendum-Navigating_beyond_COVID-19.pdf

Photo credits: Cover design on the basis of image from © ArtWell/Shutterstock.com.

Corrigenda to publications may be found on line at: www.oecd.org/about/publishing/corrigenda.htm.

Foreword

Since the COVID-19 crisis, societies have come to realise that recovery cannot mean simply returning to the way life was before the pandemic, but rather that we must "build back better". Recovery plans building on this notion provide an opportunity to design and implement much needed reforms for sustainable economic growth and more inclusive societies.

This report presents policy considerations for a post-pandemic recovery in the MENA region, reflecting in particular on the types of impacts and emerging trends in MENA economies and asking how these may modify the region's reform agendas.

The analysis was completed shortly before the start of the war in Ukraine, when signs that recovery was faltering had already been observed across the world economy. Since then, global growth prospects have been further affected by the war – and in such a way that it is too soon to fully assess the extent of the impact. The OECD estimates global economic growth could slow sharply this year, to around 3%, and remain at a similar pace in 2023 (*OECD Economic Outlook*, June 2022). Initial analysis of the impact of the war in Ukraine on the MENA region suggests that higher commodity prices risk considerably worsening the region's economic outlook.

Nevertheless, the policy considerations for building long-term resilience in MENA countries have not changed. On the contrary, this report shows that they are all the more pertinent, as many of the challenges ahead come from structural factors. MENA countries should reinforce their efforts to promote a structural reform agenda that improves economic resilience, sustainability and welfare provision, builds inclusive societies, and promote projects responding to the urgency of climate change, while capitalising on green and digital transitions. Realistic strategies also depend on fiscal affordabilty, however.

The pandemic, and now the war in Ukraine, have strengthened the rationale for co-operative solutions to address challenges that, while regional, generate global consequences. Policy reforms take place at the national level, but international co-operation is key to developing sound policy tools to help the reform process. The New Agenda for the Mediterranean of the European Union calls for transforming "the Mediterranean basin into an area of dialogue, exchange and cooperation, guaranteeing peace, stability and prosperity". MENA countries are encouraged to further strengthen their collaboration with multilateral platforms, such as the OECD and the Union for the Mediterranean, engaging with peers across the world, to benefit from the exchange of experiences and best policy practice.

It is in this spirit that this report has been prepared and we hope it will be useful to governments and civil society alike as they work to build back better in the Mediterranean.

Andreas Schaal,

Director for OECD Global Relations and Cooperation and OECD Sherpa to the G7, the G20 and APEC

Acknowledgements

This report was developed in the Global Relations and Co-operation Directorate (GRC) of the OECD, led by Andreas Schaal, Director, and benefitted from the financial support of the German Development Co-operation. It was prepared in the Middle East and Africa (MEA) Division under the strategic guidance of Carlos Conde, Head of MEA division. The drafting team, led by Mariarosa Lunati, included Jaroslaw Mrowiec, Roger Forés Carrión, Shannon Monaghan and Zoé Ryan.

The OECD is grateful to Mohammed Elrazzaz from the Union for the Mediterranean (UfM) and Johannes Laepple, Alicia Figueroa Romero and Andreas Garbade from Deutsche Gesellschaft für Internationale Zusammenarbeit (GIZ) GmbH for their useful comments to the draft report. Nevertheless, the report presents the views of the authors and does not necessarily reflect the opinions of the UfM Secretariat nor of the German Development Cooperation nor of the authorities of the countries concerned. The names used in the report to designate any territory, city or area are without prejudice to the official terminology used by the UfM Secretariat.

Two lead reviewers from the Global Relations and Co-operation directorate, William Tompson and Alexander Böhmer carefully reviewed the draft report, while Kate Lancaster, Communications Manager of the Directorate provided editorial advice. Numerous experts in the Organisation provided advice on specifc topic areas, notably from the Centre for Entrepreneurship, SMEs, Regions and Cities: Lucia Cusmano, David Halabisky, Tadashi Matsumoto, Jonathan Potter, Stephan Raes, Oriana Romano, Jane Stacey; Environment Directorate: Kathleen Dominique, Eija Kiiskinen, Deger Saygin; and the Directorate for Science, Technology and Innovation: Mario Cervantes. Finally, valuable comments were received from experts and policy makers from MENA countries who participated in seminars on recovery strategies in the MENA region where findings of the draft report were discussed.

Wendy Stokle, Communication Lead in the MEA Division, managed the production of the publication, with support from Ismail Aykin, Kamil Chehayeb, Alexandre Nachef, Maxime Ozoux, and Khaoula Yahiaoui.

Table of contents

FIGURES

TABLES

Preface by the Union for the Mediterranean

Following the launch of the first edition of the Progress Report on *Regional Integration in the UfM Region* last year, I am pleased to present the report: *Navigating beyond COVID-19 – Recovery in the MENA Region*. This report, developed by the OECD with the support of the German Development Cooperation, focuses on the COVID-19 post-pandemic recovery in the Middle-East and North Africa (MENA), which is one of the regions most adversely affected by the social and economic impacts of this health crisis.

In the current context of major global disruptions, including food insecurity and a dual energy and climate crisis, we cannot possibly talk about a meaningful recovery for the Southern and Eastern Mediterranean without a proper understanding of the existing deficits and the lost opportunities associated with the current socio-economic and environmental realities in the region. This is exactly what this publication provides.

The report, which draws on the expertise and the evidence-based approach of the OECD, does not only take stock of key emerging trends and tendencies in the region in the aftermath of the COVID-19 pandemic. It also presents sound policy considerations for a post-pandemic recovery in the different priority areas of the UfM, ranging from economic development and social affairs to water, energy and climate action.

More than just a mapping exercise of the region, the report offers valuable reflections for tangible action that can yield concrete benefits for the region. This exemplifies the UfM Secretariat's objective to use its convening power and structured methodology to build consensus on regional sectoral agendas, based on sound data, with a view to delivering value within and beyond its ecosystem. The UfM Secretariat's response to the COVID-19 crisis comes in different ways, ranging from UfM grant schemes and thematic conferences to studies and the creation of knowledge. In this spirit, I hope that this report will also support and guide your future actions in the MENA Region.

Nasser Kamel
Secretary General
Union for the Mediterranean

Executive Summary

Navigating beyond COVID-19, Recovery in the MENA Region reflects on the impacts of the COVID-19 crisis on MENA countries and the potential changes it may bring to their reform agendas. It addresses not only the ongoing effects of the crisis, but also examines long-term consequences and identifies emerging new trends.

The report suggests directions for policy action, knowing that MENA governments will need to set priorities due to limited public resources today. To increase resources, governments should continue their transitions toward a more sustainable economic model, with a competitive private sector and a business environment that attracts foreign direct investment and serves sustainable development goals.

Existing structural weaknesses of MENA economies hindered a resilient crisis response

Even before the pandemic, unemployment rates in the MENA region were among the highest in the world. In 2020, ILO Rapid Labour Force Surveys on the impact of COVID-19 revealed that among surveyed people, the unemployment rate increased 50% in Egypt, 33% in Tunisia and 23% in Morocco, further drawing attention to the labour market's structural weaknesses. The public sector accounts for large shares of formal employment in most MENA countries, but its ability to maintain and/or to create jobs was reduced by the pandemic, due to the need to allocate substantial public funds to address the socio-economic impacts of the crisis. Scarce formal employment opportunities outside the public sector led to increased informal work, already particularly high in the region.

The pandemic caused disruptions across multiple employment sectors, including tourism, a major employer in several MENA countries. Despite governments' efforts to support SMEs facing the crisis, structural problems – notably the shortage of working capital and limited access to finance – increased the vulnerability of small firms.

Trade flows from and to the MENA region fell 16% in 2020, although trade subject to regional trade agreements (RTAs) in MENA countries was often more resilient to the downturn, depending on the specific RTA and trade direction (i.e. export or import flows).

The COVID-19 crisis also put a spotlight on the MENA region's already weak health and social protection systems, as well as its weak supply chains of fundamental goods, notably food. The pressure of the pandemic on these existing weaknesses increased the risk of poverty and worsened food insecurity and malnutrition, particularly for vulnerable groups such as informal workers, women and unemployed young people. Countries that had invested in modern data and information systems for social protection programmes were more agile at scaling up of social protections and reached more people, including marginalised groups.

Restricted mobility during the pandemic fostered the use of digital tools, creating a shift toward digitalisation in education and research. In this regard, the crisis revealed the extent of the digital divide and the socio-cultural inequalities in the MENA region, especially for populations far from the urban centres.

The crisis has also highlighted the importance of thinking about sustainable models for urban space and of finding solutions to challenges such as distance to essential services or poor access to water. In the MENA region, these vulnerabilities indirectly resulted from rapid urbanisation, which often lacked sufficient provision of adequate infrastructure and services.

Pandemic-related plastic waste, such as masks and gloves, pointed to inefficient waste management systems in the MENA region, which already had systematic failures in the plastic value chain. In tandem, the decrease in air pollutants during periods of restricted mobility underlined the health costs of high exposure to air pollution associated with current models of economic and urban development in the region. Improving the governance of public transport and reduced mobility through teleworking could, in the long run, substantially reduce NO^2 pollution.

The COVID-19 crisis has exacerbated water stress in the MENA region, already the world's most water scarce area. To counteract the shortages of imported food in the early months of the pandemic, countries had to re-allocate extra water resources to agricultural production to boost local food output. This, however, further undermined the region's fragile overall water resource management (8.51 km^3/year of the region's wastewater is not reused), as it has required substantial additional investment to meet the greater water needs.

Financial difficulties and fluctuations in oil prices during the pandemic have had a negative impact on the feasibility and/or attractiveness of green energy solutions in the MENA countries. The costs of energy price volatility confirmed, however, the fundamental need for stable, renewable and resilient energy sources for the MENA region.

The pandemic also highlighted the central role of R&D in providing scientific and technical solutions to mitigate the negative effects of COVID-19 and in fields important for the MENA region, such as climate change and water scarcity. This has led to deeper regional appreciation for the value of international collaboration in research and encouraged public-private partnerships.

Policy considerations for a sound recovery and sustainable growth

To build a sustainable, resilient and inclusive recovery, MENA countries are encouraged to:

- Address the structural weaknesses of the labour market and capitalise on new economic trends for maintaining and creating employment.
- Further digitalise the education system for long-term resilience and more inclusiveness.
- Help young people and women access new learning and job opportunities by boosting digital skills and infrastructure.
- Foster a culture of entrepreneurship and private sector development that encourages the formalisation of informal activities.
- Capitalise on new travel behaviours induced by the pandemic, away from busy tourist hotspots to proximity tourism and less air travel.
- Deepen scientific co-operation at the regional level and increase the investment in R&D.
- Increase investment jobs in the water sectors, and include environmental fiscal reforms in policy agendas.
- Promote public and private initiatives on green and resilient urban mobility in order to maintain new mobility habits and reduce pollution levels.
- Build public-private partnerships in order to mobilise the private sector financing needed for resilient energy infrastructure systems.
- Enhance regional environmental co-ordination in order to prevent biodiversity loss, which can be a driver of infectious diseases.

Russia's aggression against Ukraine and impacts in the MENA region

This report was prepared before Russia's large scale aggression against the Ukraine. Nevertheless, it is important to add a preliminary analysis on the impact the war will have in the MENA region[1].

While the war is relatively distant from the region's borders, MENA countries are expected to experience a significant economic impact as the conflict disrupts the region's supply chains for food imports, on which most MENA countries depend, and alters global energy prices (Figure 1).

Figure 1. More than one third of MENA imports relate to food and fuel and their share had increased during the pandemic

Left axis: Billions of USD; right axis: % of total exports

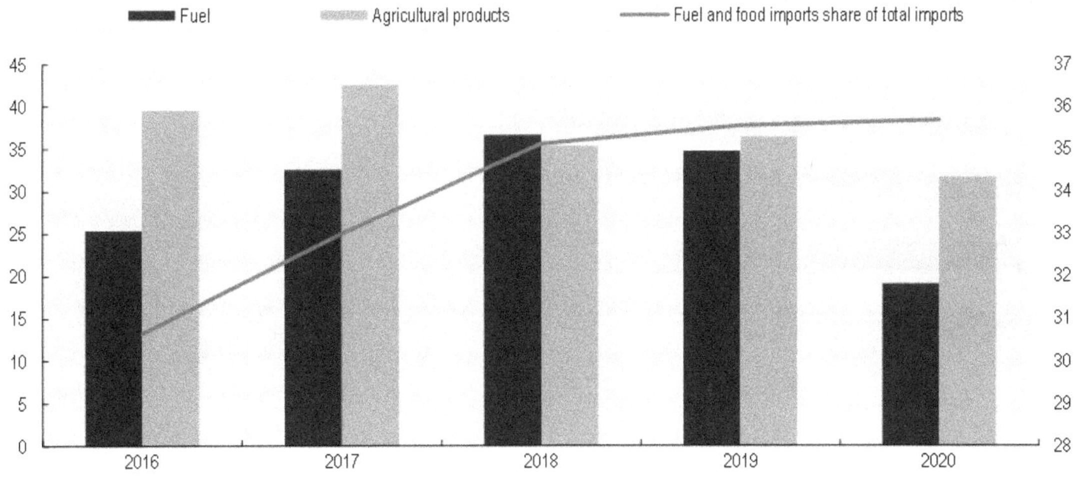

Source: OECD calculations, UN Comtrade Database.

Fuel imports. As Russia is one of the largest producers and exporters of hydrocarbons, production and supply disruptions, as well as the sanctions imposed on Russia, have major effects on oil, gas and fuel prices. These have already seen a significant increase since 2021, after an initial decrease at the beginning of the pandemic.

The search for alternatives to Russian sources of hydrocarbons could benefit MENA producers in the medium to long term. Replacing Russia's oil and gas exports to Europe would require both addressing investments to boost local production and building new intra-regional infrastructures, in particular for the more complex logistics for gas, which cannot possibly be achieved in the short-term. Sustained high oil and gas prices may also contribute to inflation and/or stressed public budgets through increased energy subsidies. According to the IEA, in 2020 Algeria's average energy subsidisation rate was 52%, representing USD 191 per capita and 5.8% of GDP; and Egypt's average energy subsidisation rate was 29%, representing USD 77 per capita and 2.2% of GDP. For oil importing MENA countries, high energy prices will have substantial impacts in fiscal budgets, trade balances and hard currency reserves, contributing to economic and social instability.

Food imports. MENA countries imported in 2020 over 30 billion USD on agricultural products and food. This represented 22% of the region's total imports of goods and remained the most relevant category in the import basket. Russia and Ukraine are major producers of staple foods (cereals) around the world, accounting for around 30% of the world's wheat exports and 14 % of maize exports, as well as more than 50% of sunflower seed oil. Russia (and Belarus, which is also being subject to sanctions) are also major producers of fertilisers.

Many MENA countries are particularly reliant on agricultural imports from Russia and Ukraine. For example, Lebanon imports 60% of its wheat from Ukraine, and Egypt imports nearly 85% from Russia and Ukraine, Tunisia over 47% from the two countries, with a high very reliance on Ukraine, Morocco imports nearly a quarter and Jordan imports over 34% from these countries (Figure 2).

Figure 2. Wheat imports from Russia and Ukraine by country, 2020

Percentage of total wheat imports

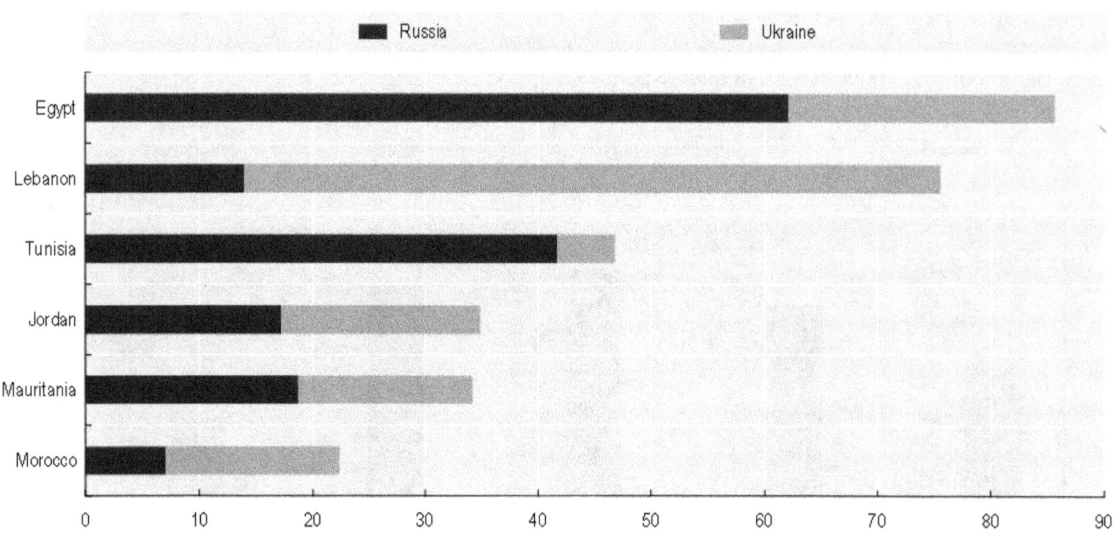

Note: Algeria's and the Palestinian Authority's wheat imports from Russia and Ukraine in 2020 were negligible.
Source: OECD calculations, UN Comtrade database.

The MENA region has one of the highest rates of food insecurity in the world. Given the dependency on food imports, the war in Ukraine is likely to increase food insecurity in the region. The number of food insecure people inthe MENA countries has steadily increased during the first 3 months of the war, from 26 million in February to 28.3 in May 2022[2].

Migration. Lastly, possible effects also concern movements of people from MENA to the Northern shore of the Mediterranean. Important flows of Ukrainian refugees are currently being relocated across Europe. In the near future, this could have an impact on the opportunities to work and study in European countries for people of other geographical areas.

Box 1. Overview of impact of the war in Ukraine in MENA countries. A preliminary assessment

Despite the common challenges countries in the MENA region are facing, analysis at the country level will be necessary to asses properly the impact of the war. Preliminary findings are summarised below.

Algeria traditionally has not relied heavily on food imports from Ukraine or Russia[a]. However, the country is exposed to higher food prices due to global markets fluctuations. Algeria, which was already facing a surge in prices since 2021, will most likely continue expanding its efforts to prevent basic food goods inflation. This will require increasing public expenditure in a context of budgetary resource rationalisation, which has been a relevant goal of the government since the start of the pandemic. Unlike other neighbouring countries, Algeria's increased hydrocarbon revenues, due to the international oil price surge, will facilitate the government's plans to reduce the inflation's short-term impact but may delay the implementation of budget rationalisation reforms.

Egypt, the world's largest wheat importer, heavily relies on Ukraine and Russia for meeting its national cereal needs and is a net importer of other essential basic food items, such as cooking oils. In this context, soaring prices, the drop of tourism from Ukraine and Russia -a significant source of foreign currency - and the increasing investment outflows, forced Egypt to request assistance to the IMF in March 2022. The IMF's external financing is expected to help the country to address inflation, while maintaining its foreign reserves and implementing a debt rationalisation programme starting in 2022.

Jordan has managed to contain inflation below 2% during the past year but the impact of the conflict in Ukraine is yet to be assessed. As a net importer of basic food goods and fuel, it is to be expected that Jordan's households and public accounts will be further stressed due to rising food and oil prices and reduced tourism flows caused by a drop in the global purchasing power. In this context, Jordan will most likely increase public debt, already rising since the pandemic's onset, increasing interest rates and furthering currency devaluation.

Lebanon is expected to be among the MENA countries most affected by the war in Ukraine. Lebanon heavily relies on wheat imports from Ukraine and is a net oil importer. As the country is still suffering the consequences of the fuel crisis in 2021, heavy inflation and currency devaluation, and shortages in supermarkets, additional prices stress in basic goods and those services which very much depend on oil costs (such as transport or electricity generation) will most likely exacerbate the economic collapse and increase food insecurity. Lebanon is currently discussing with the IMF a four-year extended fund facility to support the country's stabilisation.

In **the Palestinian Authority,** wheat costs have increased over 25% since the war started, and other food goods have also seen a significant increase in prices, which heavily affected local households' purchasing power. According to the WFP, food insecurity has reached 31.2% (64% in Gaza, 9% in West Bank). Also, without specific measures, wheat reserves could be soon exhausted (less than a month according to Oxfam; 2-3 months according to the Ministry of National Economy).

Morocco has a strong agricultural sector, which includes wheat production, albeit insufficient to meet the internal demand. Traditionally, the country has imported around 20% of its wheat needs from Ukraine and Russia. While the economic performance of the country will depend more on the demand of European countries of Morocco's manufactured products, inflationary food and oil prices will nonetheless affect the country's households and economic activities, limiting growth prospects for 2022.

In **Tunisia**, inflation reached 7.2% in March 2022, in year-to-year basis, the highest level in three years. Similarly to other food-importers-non-oil producers from the region, Tunisia is particularly sensible to oil and food price fluctuations. The current crisis may exacerbate Tunisia's feeble economic prospects, which remained weak for the last decade -and were worsened by the pandemic. Under a scenario of low employment generation and high unemployment, Tunisia is working with the IMF to expand the current help to tackle the effects of the pandemic to face the worsened scenario caused by the war.

a. Over the past years, Algeria planned to significantly increase its wheat imports from Russia, to become by 2022 the main source for the country, https://www.reuters.com/article/algeria-wheat-russia-idAFL5N2O435X

Sources: Comtrade data; IMF; World Bank; national administrations.

Notes

[1] MENA region or MENA countries refer to the group of countries that are members of the Union for the Mediterranean. These countries are: Algeria, Egypt, Jordan, Lebanon, Mauritania, Morocco, Palestinian Authority and Tunisia. Where the term "broad MENA region" is used, it refers to the group of MENA countries that include UfM and non-UfM members.

[2] Source: WFP HungerMap^{LIVE}. Includes data from two sources: (1) WFP's continuous, near real-time monitoring systems, which remotely collect thousands of data daily through live calls conducted by call centres around the world; and (2) machine learning-based predictive models.

1 Economic development and employment

This chapter discusses the impacts of COVID-19 on employment and the business sector, in particular small and medium-sized enterprises, in the MENA region. It reflects on the vulnerabilities caused by the significant share of informality in the economies of the region and highlights the effects of the pandemic on tourism and trade. It also examines policy approaches to address the challenges of a sustainable and inclusive recovery.

Key takeaways

- The MENA region has among the highest unemployment rates in the world. The outbreak of the COVID-19 pandemic has further increased unemployment and highlighted the need to address the structural weaknesses of the labour market to ensure a sustainable recovery and build resilience to face future crises. This goal can be achieved through coordinated initiatives that encompass private sector development, supporting SMEs, accompanying the transformation of sustainable tourism and strengthening trade including through participation in GVCs.
- The public sector currently represents large shares of total formal employment in the MENA countries. Yet in the context of the COVID-19 pandemic, its ability to create and/or maintain jobs has been limited, due to the substantial allocation of public funds to address the socio-economic impacts of the crisis. The scarcity of formal employment opportunities outside the public sector has increased informal activities during the pandemic.
- In the region, as elsewhere in the world, a significant portion of private sector formal employment is driven by SMEs. Despite government efforts to support SMEs during the pandemic, various constraints on SME growth, e.g. limited access to finance and use of digital tools, restrained their performance as a factor of resilience. A better entrepreneurial ecosystem would provide a path to recovery. In this process, it would be particularly crucial to ensure the mobilisation, inclusion and empowerment of youth and women in the economy.
- The COVID-19 pandemic highlighted the fragility of trade linkages in the MENA region. At the global level, it was observed that countries having Regional Trade Agreements (RTAs) experienced, on average, a lower decline in trade (8.5%-11.2%) compared to countries that lacked them (14.1%). This positive dynamic could be observed as well with regard to MENA region's RTAs, although with differences depending on the specific RTA and trade direction i.e. export or import flows. While exports between Agadir and PAFTA/GAFTA signatory countries experienced a lesser drop of intra-region exports than the drop of exports to other partners, imports, on the contrary, fell more sharply between the RTAs adherents. Trade between the EU and MENA countries with Association Agreements showed in most cases resilience in 2020, both for imports and exports.
- Sustainability is becoming more prominent in tourism choices, due to greater awareness of climate change and the impact of tourism on it. Tourism is an increasingly important sector for the MENA region, accounting for above or close to 10% of GDP and close to 7% of employment in some countries before the pandemic. The crisis has modified travel behaviour, in particular away from busy tourist hotspots to proximity tourism, associated with a decline in air travel. In the long term, this trend could create new opportunities for the travel and tourism sector in MENA countries, as it drives new business models and markets and opens up employment possibilities. MENA countries could benefit from domestic tourism and further develop regional tourism across both shores of the Mediterranean, promoting cultural and economic developments in the region, while making the tourism sector more sustainable and resilient.

Employment

The outbreak of the COVID-19 pandemic further intensified structural weaknesses of the labour market in the MENA region[1], i.e. pervasive informality and a large share of the public sector employment. The labour market participation rate is much lower in the region than in other parts of the world, notably because of the low rates of formal employment of women. Overall, women's labour force participation in the region is only 21% compared to 70% for men (Figure 1.1).

Figure 1.1. Female labour force participation rate, 2010-19

% of female population aged 15+

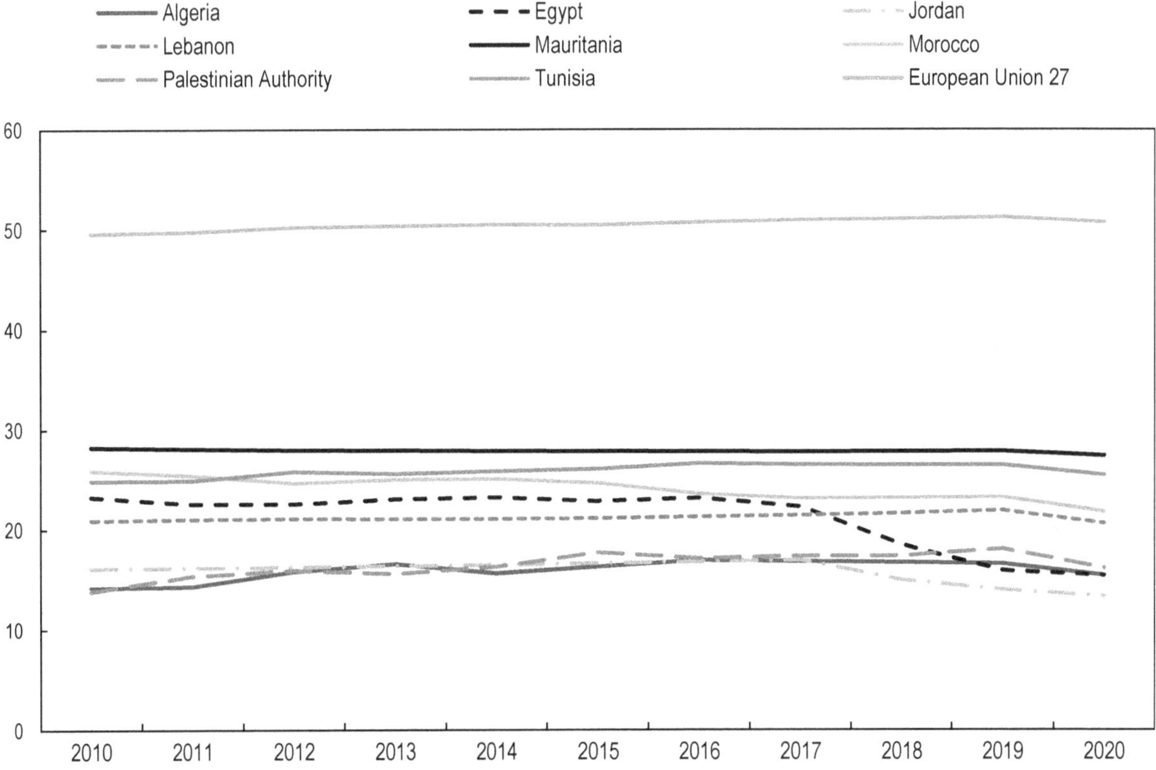

Note: Labour force participation rate is the proportion of the population aged 15 and older that is economically active: all people who supply labour for the production of goods and services during a specified period. This is a modeled ILO estimate. The series is part of the ILO estimates and is harmonized to ensure comparability across countries and over time by accounting for differences in data source, scope of coverage, methodology, and other country-specific factors. The estimates are based mainly on nationally representative labor force surveys, with other sources (population censuses and nationally reported estimates) used only when no survey data are available. Estimates for countries with very limited labour market information have a high degree of uncertainty. Hence, estimates for countries with limited nationally reported data should not be considered as "observed" data, and great care needs to be applied when using these data for analysis, especially at the country level.
Source: International Labour Organization, ILOSTAT database. https://ilostat.ilo.org/data/.

The size of the public sector in the region, a strong employment provider, tends to be bigger than in other middle-income and emerging economies, although, for some countries it has slighlty declined over time. The public sector wage bill in the MENA region ranges between 4.7% of the GDP (Jordan) to 14.1% (Tunisia), with Algeria, Lebanon, and Morocco also over 10%. Public wages in most emerging economies tend to represent a smaller share of the GDP (2.6% for Kazakhastan, 5.1% for Colombia, 5.4% for

Indonesia), yet, other major emerging economies such as Brazil and South Africa devote significant resources to public workers (World Bank, 2021[1]). Rapid labour force surveys conducted during the first year of the pandemic revealed a significant increase of unemployment rates among surveyed individuals, reaching an increase of 50% in the case of Egypt, 33% in Tunisia and 23% in Morocco[2]. In the context of the COVID-19 pandemic, with raising unemployment, the public sector was no longer in a position to create, or even maintain, jobs, due to the considerable fiscal efforts for supporting national economies from the economic and social impact of the crisis.

Some initiatives exist, such as the reinstatement of compulsory military service in Jordan to limit youth unemployment, but in absolute terms the contraction of the public employment market highlights the necessity of taking action to create more employment opportunities in the private sector.[3]

COVID-19 and informality

The MENA region has one of the highest rates of informal employment in the world; notably, on average 68% of employment in the region is informal (OECD, 2020[2]). Informality is generally associated with limited to no social protection coverage and low and unstable incomes, making informal workers particularly vulnerable in times of crisis (World Bank, 2021[3]). During the COVID-19 pandemic, social distancing and confinement measures reinforced the vulnerabilities of informal workers in MENA economies, where they are largely concentrated in low-productivity jobs requiring physical presence, with no possibility of working remotely. During the COVID-19 crisis, mobility restrictions have therefore further burdened the activity of informal workers, who faced the dilemma of complying with health measures or maintaining a source of income to meet their basic expenses (OECD, 2020[2]).

While COVID-19 did still contribute to the further development of informality, which is on an upward curve in the MENA region, ad-hoc mobility restrictions, limited role of informality as a crisis-times buffer against negative shocks by temporarily absorbing labour pushed out of the formal sector. This is particularly the case in the economies where regulatory efforts seem to have contained its diffusion (OECD, 2021[4]).

Because of the monitoring difficulties associated with the informal sector's hidden nature, many informal workers experienced greater difficulty in benefiting from the Government's pandemic emergency packages (World Bank, 2021[5]). To partially address the absence of official data, MENA countries implemented specific measures to support informal workers, through for example, cash transfers addressed to households (OECD, 2020[2]). Nearly 62% of all female workers are informally employed in the broad MENA region (ILO data) (OECD, 2020[6]). Within the informal employment sphere, women are typically the most vulnerable and lowest paid category, employed heavily in services, especially tourism, agriculture and domestic work. The presence and patterns of women in the informal economy in the region are linked to interrelated socio-economic, cultural, structural and institutional factors. In addition, household chores, coupled with the often limited availability of affordable childcare facilities and family-friendly policies, act as a brake on women's employment (OECD, 2021[7]). Due to those regional-specific barriers related to unequal economic opportunities, women's job and income security are more exposed to the economic fallout from the pandemic.

The impact of the pandemic on employment highlights the necessity for governments to facilitate the transition of the labour force away from informality and towards creating more opportunities in the private sector. Governments will need to find additional revenues to finance the significant costs of relief efforts to mitigate the adverse effects of the global pandemic on their economies. This is especially true given the limited tax base in the broad MENA region and the high levels of unemployment and informality. The following sections consider respectively the potential of SMEs, trade and tourism as gateways to economic growth, sustainable development and decent jobs.

SMEs

As virtually everywhere around the world, SMEs also play a central role in MENA economies constituting the majority of business units and accounting for significant shares of jobs.

- SMEs play a substantial role in formal employment in the private sector in Egypt (around 33%), Jordan (around 43%), Lebanon (55%), Morocco (nearly 30%), the Palestinian Authority (over 90%) and Tunisia (nearly 40%) (OECD, 2020[2]).

Moreover, formal and informal micro enterprises, i.e. businesses with fewer than 10 employed persons, and self-employed account for 70% of total employment in the region, just behind South Asia and Sub-Saharan Africa, both with a share of 80% (OECD, 2020[2]). MENA countries are fully aware of the importance of SMEs and have put in place strategies to encourage and support entrepreneurship. Reforms are at varying stages of progress, starting with the incorporation of SME issues into national development plans or broad strategies, e.g. Algeria, Jordan, Morocco and Tunisia. Some countries already adopted dedicated SME strategies and laws, notably Egypt, Lebanon and Morocco. These countries also recognise that many SMEs operate in the informal sector and are making efforts to reduce informality in their economies, (IMF, 2019[8]) by for example encouraging informal-sector business owners to formalise their jobs and benefit from targetted services on financing, training and mentoring.

As a result of the COVID-19 crisis, a significant proportion of SMEs in the broad MENA region had to reduce their permanent employment, if not completely shut down. The persistent decline in business activities and the duration of the pandemic increases the risks of permanent job loss for MENA firms. For instance, in Jordan, during the early stage of the pandemic (i.e. July-August 2020), 26% of firms reduced their permanent workers; they were 39% to do so in the period November 2020-January 2021 (ILO, 2021[9]).

Governments of MENA countries have implemented numerous initiatives to support SMEs against the COVID-19 crisis -for a deeper analysis on initiatives in Egypt and Tunisia, see (OECD, 2021[10]). However, structural weaknesses of the business environment (Figure 1.2) and their reflex on the typical characteristics of the business population, made it more difficult for SMEs in the region to face the pandemic. In particular:

- *Insufficient access to finance.* A smaller proportion of SMEs have a loan or line of credit than large enterprises: only 8% of debt goes to SMEs in the broad MENA region. This is lower than the average of 18% for middle-income countries and 22% for high-income countries. Nearly 63% of MENA MSMEs lack access to finance and the total financing gap for MSMEs in the region is estimated at USD210-240 billion (of which the formal MSME financing gap is estimated at USD180-160 billion) (IFC, 2021[11]). These difficulties seem to be rooted in the lack of an adequate enabling environment, which referes to a lack of sufficient regulation (such as simplyfing licensing requirements, facilitating market access for regional and international etc.), poor financial infrastructure, and often the absence of suitable banking products.
- *Limited use of digital tools.* While some SMEs operating in a number of sectors, notably the retail sector, have been able to maintain their activity thanks to digital tools, a good share of SMEs in the broad MENA region were not yet equipped with the digitalisation of business processes and functions. Prior to the pandemic, only 8% of SMEs in the broad MENA region had an online presence (compared to 80% in the United States) and only 1.5% of the region's retailers were online (OECD, 2021[12]).

Figure 1.2. Top business environment constraints in the MENA region

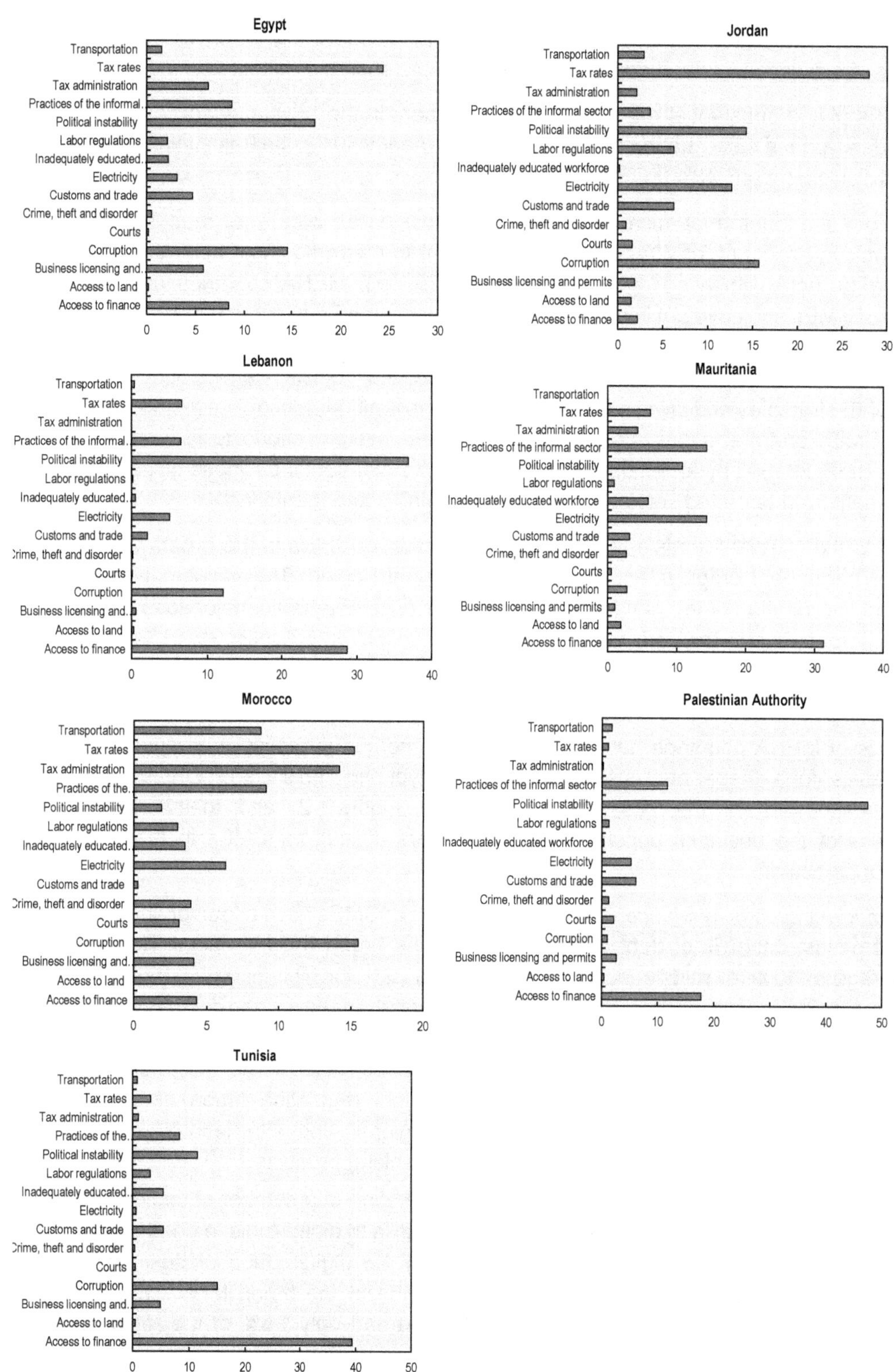

Note: Percentage of firms that consider a given business environment obstacle as the most important one from a list of 15 business environment obstacles. The figure presents the top ranking obstacles compared to the regional averages. Data for Egypt and Tunisia refer to 2020 ; for Jordan, Lebanon, Morocco, the Palestinian Authority, to 2019; for Mauritania, to 2014. Data for Algeria are not available
Source: World Bank Enterprise Survey (WBES) (2020), https://www.enterprisesurveys.org/en/enterprisesurveys.

- *Vulnerability of women-led businesses.* Several characteristics of respectively women- and men-owned enterprises affected their resilience to the COVID-19 crisis. In particular, women-owned businesses are more likely than men-owned to operate in services sectors that were severely hit by the pandemic-induced demand shock, e.g. retail trade, hospitality, personal services (OECD, 2020[2]). The lower resilience of women-led businesses in the region is further compounded by the average lower size of these businesses, which also tend to have younger employees and managers. Because of this, women-led businesses are more likely to be self-financed, or financed by friends and family, and have fewer financial assets. In the region, as it happens in other parts of the world, access to credit is easier for businesses owned by men, preferably with previous work experience and collaterals. Conversely, also due to societal considerations, young women entrepreneurs find it more difficult to access traditional financing. Moreover, in the broad MENA region only 38% of women have a bank account, compared to 57% of men (OECD, 2020[13]). Finally, women entrepreneurs have fewer networks of professional contacts to exchange advice on managing the pandemic, and also lower levels of digital connectivity that could have helped them to face and adapt to market disruptions (IFC, 2021[14]).
- Beyond these vulnerabilities, the broad MENA region has one of the lowest share of women-owned SMEs in the world. Data from 2019 estimate that only 14%, compared to the global average of 34% (OECD/ILO/CAWTAR, 2020[15]). The under-exploited potential of female entrepreneurship is considered a factor that lowers resilience in times of crises (World Bank, 2021[16]).

However, despite adverse factors, *start-ups are already helping build resilience of MENA economies.* According to data by MAGNiTT, a consultancy based in Dubai, MENA start-ups in 2020 saw a record USD 1 billion in investments, up 13% from 2019, while the number of investment deals decreased. This positive trend also continued in 2021, with start-ups rising and 862 million USD in Q2 2021 (MAGNiTT, 2021[17]). In the MENA region, Egypt is the most dynamic, being one of three main hubs in the broad MENA region, along with Saudi Arabia and the United Arab Emirates. In 2021, these three countries alone attracted 71% of the capital dedicated to start-ups in the Middle East. The sectors benefiting most from high investment are fintech, e-commerce (in the broadest sense of the term, which also includes the transport of goods traded electronically), ED-tech and health (WAMDA, 2021[18]).

Policy considerations

Strengthening the resilience of the region's SMEs ecosystem and facilitating an inclusive recovery ready for the challenges of the digital economy should take into account major policy considerations:

- *Promote a more inclusive private sector for disaster response and post-disaster reconstruction.* Governments will need to find additional revenues to finance the significant costs of relief efforts to mitigate the adverse effects of the global pandemic on their economies. This is especially true given the limited tax base in the broad MENA region, related to the high levels of informality. Investing in the resilience of SMEs and the private sector in general is an economic imperative for the MENA region. This involves lifting existing constraints on business development to foster growth of inclusive and competitive SMEs that can contribute to employment opportunities in the region. Leveraging the role of the private sector will also require facilitating the accessibility of public support packages and creating harmonised and transparent channels of communication between both sectors.
- *Create incentives to formalise the informal sector.* Governments can build on existing COVID-19 initiatives to enable a healthier environment for SMEs. For example, by improving awareness of the benefits of formalisation, simplifying administrative procedures, reducing tax compliance costs, and addressing the skills gap of informal economy workers.
    - The Palestinian Authority launched an SME fund to provide soft loans to SMEs and a credit facility of USD 32 million was extended to SMEs (IMF, 2021[19]); Jordan expanded

the guarantees provided by the Jordanian Loan Guarantee Cooperation on SME loans, including credit facilities made available for the tourist sector (Central Bank of Jordan, 2020[20]); Lebanon launched a USD 797 million stimulus package aimed at supporting daily workers in the public sector, health care workers and farmers and subsidized loans for SMEs (OECD, 2020[2]).

- *Support broader adoption of digital tools by their SMEs ecosystem* by addressing the main barriers behind SME digitalisation efforts. This includes working on institutional and regulatory gaps (e.g. launch e-government platforms; define clear digitalisation strategies; create incentives for SMEs to digitalise such as including online invoicing), promote specific training on digitalisation for local public officials, mentors, business organisations and youth, expand the development of digital infrastructure (e.g. internet connectivity) and promote specific digital innovation hubs (European Union, 2020[21]).
- *Enable the delivery of adequate support and training for entrepreneurs, and offer opportunities for MSMEs to adapt their operating modes and business models to the new environment*, improving digital education and acquisition of soft and hard digital skills. Digital literacy plays an essential role in fostering employability in the private sector and in formal entrepreneurship. Examples of public efforts to increase the region's readiness to capitalise on the digital economy already exist. Egypt's digital strategy, launched in 2020 to support its digital capacity, presents a three-pillar approach that targets the improvement of the country's digital infrastructure, its regulatory environment and promotes activities in support of skills development and innovation.

Tourism

The COVID-19 crisis severely affected the tourism sector in MENA countries, wreaking havoc on social and economic affairs of major cities and tourist sites. Tourism is a highly significant economic sector for the region, accounting for above or close to 10% of GDP and close to 7% of employment in several countries (Figure 1.3). International tourist arrivals to the Middle East declined on par with the global rate, at approximately 70% in 2020 compared to the previous year (UNWTO, 2020[22]).

Figure 1.3. Travel and tourism in the MENA region

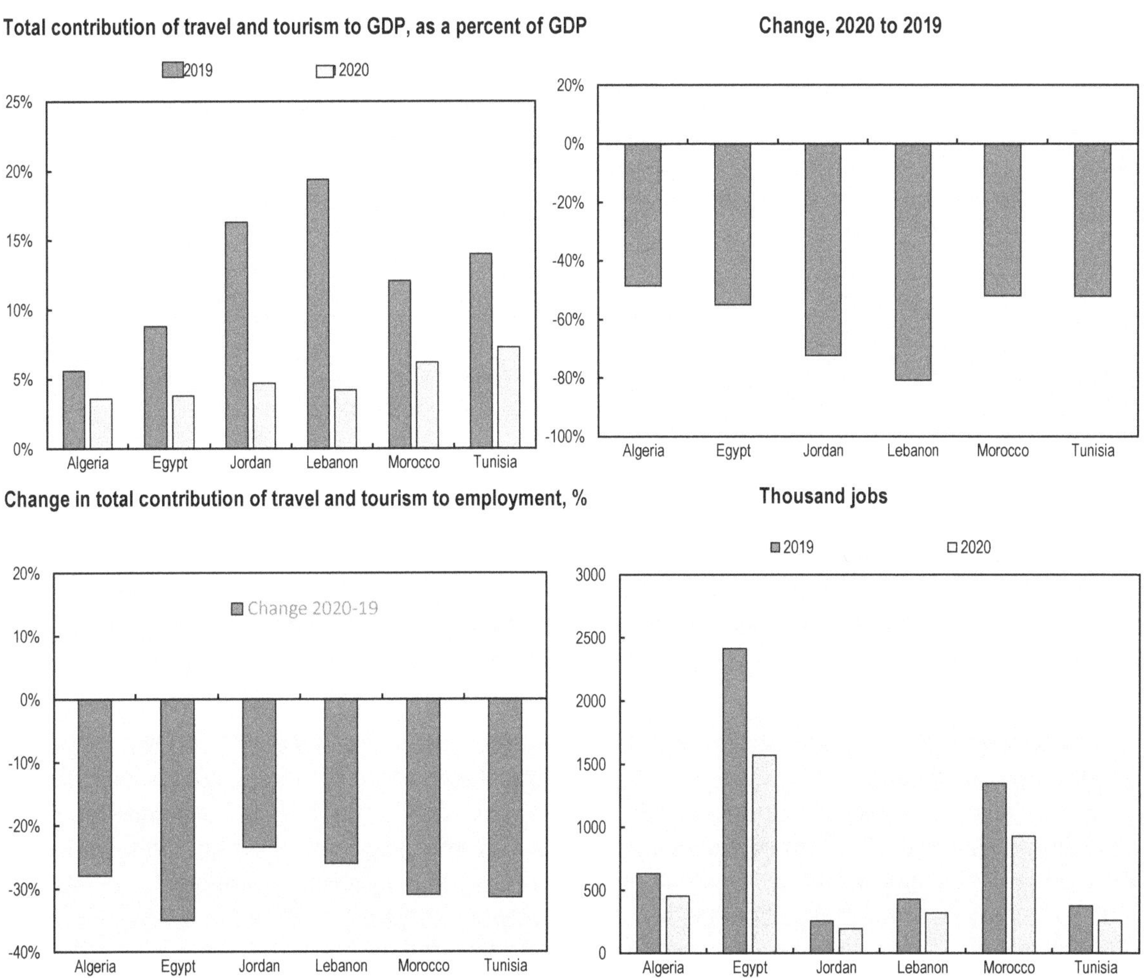

Note: Data for the Palestinian Authority and Mauritania are not available. WTTC data are model estimates, figures do not always align with country data

Source: World Travel and Tourism Council, 2021, https://wttc.org/Research/Economic-Impact

Table 1.1. Covid-19 and the travel and tourism sector in the MENA region

Drop in revenues, percentage of GDP and number of jobs, 2019-20

	% drop in revenues from travel and tourism sectors	% drop of travel and tourism sectors of GDP	% decline in travel and tourism jobs
Algeria	-49.1%	-49.1 % [From 10.4% of GDP in 2019 to 5.5% in 2020]	-18.5 % From 334 thousands jobs in 2019 to 272 million jobs in 2020
Egypt	-55 %	-55 % [From 8.8 % of GDP in 2019 to 3.8 % in 2020]	-35% From 2.4 million in 2019 to 1.6 million in 2020
Jordan	-80% (during the first eight months of 2020)	-72.3% [From 16.3 % of GDP in 2019 to 4.7% in 2020]	-23.4% From 255 thousands in 2019 to 196 thousands in 2020
Lebanon	-80.9 %	-78.4% [From 19.4% of GDP in 2019 to 4.2 % in 2020]	-26% From 430 thousands in 2019 to 318 thousands in 2020
Morocco	-52 %	-52 % [From 12% of GDP in 2019 to 6.2 % in 2020]	-31% From 1.35 million in 2019 to 930 000 in 2020

	% drop in revenues from travel and tourism sectors	% drop of travel and tourism sectors of GDP	% decline in travel and tourism jobs
Palestinian Authority	-68%	From 2.5% of GDP in 2019 to 1.7 % in 2020	
Tunisia	-52 %	-52 % [From 14 % of GDP in 2019 to 7.3 % in 2020]	-31.3% From 380 thousands in 2019 to 260 thousands in 2020
Worldwide	Loss of almost USD 4 trillion Loss of USD 1.3 trillion on total export revenues from international tourism -85% less tourist arrivals between 2020 and 2021	From 10.4% of GDP in 2019 to 5.5 % in 2020	-18.5% In 2020, 62 million jobs were lost From 334 million in 2019 to 272 million in 2020

Note: Data for Mauritania are not available.
Source: (WTTC, 2021[23]); (Egyptian Cabinet IDSC, 2020[24]); World Bank, 2021, Travel and Tourism direct contribution to employment https://tcdata360.worldbank.org/indicators/tot.direct.emp?country=BRA&indicator=24644&viz=line_chart&years=1995,2028; Central Bank of Jordan, 2021, https://www.cbj.gov.jo/Pages/viewpage.aspx?pageID=93

Covid-19 possibly induced short-term to longer-term travel and tourism changes. Regional and rural coastal destinations fared better than cities in terms of maintaining tourism during the pandemic, a trend that is likely to continue (OECD, 2020[25]). Changing traveller behaviour and ways of travel may lead to new opportunities for the travel and tourism sector in the MENA countries, driving innovation, new business models and niches/markets, opening up new destinations and creating more sustainable and resilient tourism.

MENA countries face important environmental challenges. With the lifting of lockdown measures demand for travel and tourism grew again, helping to mitigate the impact on jobs and businesses in some places and is likely to continue. However, due to continuing crises, there is an ongoing decline in businesses and jobs in the tourism sector with implications for travel behaviour. Coastal tourism for the MENA countries is highly reliant on environmental well-being and existing environmental challenges plaguing the region can negatively affect the successful growth of MENA tourism sectors. Water scarcity in the region will likely increase competition and tension between tourism and other sectors as tourism is a water-intensive industry. Meanwhile, desalination processes, which are necessary for water-scarce countries that rely on tourism as an important economic sector, remains expensive. Rising seas are expected to continue affecting beach-based tourism and coastal areas (C. Michael Hall, 2019[26]). Extreme events, such as heatwaves, floods and droughts also appear to be increasing in the broad MENA region, affecting not only tourism but everyday life for citizens.

The "confinement fatigue", induced by repeated confinements, shifts tourism away from busy tourist hotspots to **proximity tourism**. People prefer places with lower human density and the opportunity to emerge into local communities by working in the countryside, learning new skills and disconnecting for a while. (Southan, 2021[27]). Thus, there is a tendency for 'private solutions' when travelling, avoiding big gatherings, and prioritising private means of transport. Demand for local and smaller accommodations is expected to increase. MENA countries should exploit this opportunity to promote, through investment and promotion, rural or remote areas that were not previously privileged destinations. In this sense, the revival of tourism in the region brings the prospect of cultural and economic development of regions across the Mediterranean.

Sustainability is becoming more prominent in tourism choices due to greater climate change awareness and the impacts of tourism (OECD, 2020[25]). Therefore, shorter travel destinations may be preferred which can also impact spending patterns, as domestic tourists tend to be more price sensitive (OECD, 2020[25]). The MENA region would benefit from developing regional tourism. So far, only a small proportion of tourists from the MENA countries travel intra-regionally.

Travelling by plane travel is on decline, as travellers tend to fly to locations and then continue by 'low travel', which is using other means of travel on the ground such as trains, cars and bikes (Barry, 2021[28]). Moreover, the duration of holidays is expected to increase in the near future, as workers were saving their holidays in 2020 and waiting for less strict measures. The average trip duration in 2021 was around two weeks (Southan, 2021[27]). The increase in duration of holidays is also in line with people's prioritisation of immersing themselves into local environments.

Changes in the supply of tourism

There are several structural changes expected in tourism supply across the ecosystem:

Labour and skills shortages in the tourism sector may be exacerbated, as jobs are lost and workers redeploy to different sectors (OECD, 2020[25]) (Table 1.1). As there is reduced investment, there is a need for policies to incentivise and restore investments in the tourism sector to maintain the quality of tourism offers and promote a sustainable recovery.

COVID-19 accelerated the digitalisation of tourism services, including a higher use of automation, contact-less payments and services, virtual experiences and real-time information provision (OECD, 2020[25]). Tourism policy will need to be more reactive and is expected to move to more flexible systems over the long-term which are more quickly adaptable to changes of policy focus. Particular areas of focus will be crisis management, safety and health policy issues among others.

Policy considerations

In order to enhance the recovery of the tourism industry and promote a more inclusive and sustainable expansion of the sector, MENA countries in cooperation with regional and international actors could take the following considerations into account:

- *Exploit the shift towards proximity tourism through investment and promotion of rural or remote areas* in MENA countries that were not previously privileged destinations. In this sense, the revival of tourism in the region brings the prospect of cultural and economic development.
- *Incentivise and restore investments in the tourism sector. Labour and* skills shortages in the tourism sector were exacerbated as jobs were lost and workers redeployed to different sectors (OECD, 2020[25]). As there is reduced investment, there is a need for policies that will restore and expand investment in the tourism sector to maintain and further improve the quality of tourism and promote a sustainable recovery.
- *Develop regional tourism to expand travel flights and routes within the Mediterranean.* So far, only a small proportion of tourists from the MENA countries travel intra-regionally. There is a strong potential to exploit this post-pandemic shift and attract tourism into the broad region from outside the MENA region. Once implemented, this can be further promoted through innovative advertising and campaigns, drawing attention to the hidden cultural gems and benefits of the region.
- *Invest and improve travel infrastructure and regional cooperation.* The establishment of effective intra-regional modes of transportation would allow for a larger inflow of people moving within the region, creating further opportunities for jobs and economic development. In the long run, the aspiration for the MENA region would be to implement good practices and enhance seamless travel, an objective strongly inspired by the SDGs, which would further support the tourism industry sustainably and contribution to inclusive economic growth (OECD, 2020[29]).
- *Continue to build on the advances in digitalisation of tourism services already accelerated by the pandemic.* The pandemic has inspired a rapid move towards automation, contact-less payment and services, virtual experiences and real-time information provision (OECD, 2020[25]). Tourism policy will need to be more reactive and move to more flexible systems which are more quickly

adaptable to changes of policy focus. Particular areas of focus will be crisis management, safety and health policy issues, among others.

Trade

Trade in the MENA region has been historically defined by the considerable size of the European market (Figure 1.4), which has represented since 2006, on average, 46% of MENA countries' exports and 39% of imports. This dominance has nevertheless slowly decreased in favour of other regions of the world, and intra-MENA trade, which only suffered a considerable drop in the share in 2020.

Figure 1.4. MENA's trade volume with the EU, the MENA region and the rest of the world

% of total trade (imports and exports)

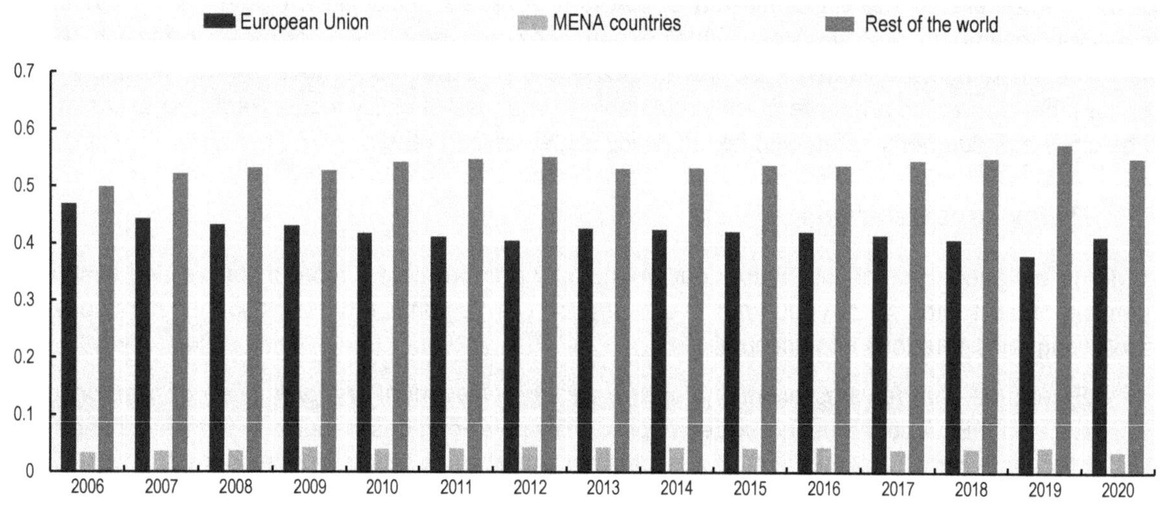

Note: Data for Algeria for 2018, 2019 and 2020, and for Tunisia for 2020 are mirrored data from reporting countries.
Source: OECD calculations, UN Comtrade database.

In the early 2000s, trade within the MENA region and between MENA countries and the rest of the world shows a similar relationship as per main commodity groups (Figure 1.5). The oil industry dominated the region's trade (imports and exports) and with the rest of the world, representing roughly 52% of the trade between MENA countries and 46% of MENA countries' trade with the rest of the world. Trade in manufactured goods was nonetheless relevant, but more present in trade between MENA and non-MENA countries.

As the decade progressed, intra-MENA and MENA's global trade slightly diverged. As such, MENA trade with the rest of the world in manufactured goods increased its share, representing by 2020 more than half of the region's trade outside its borders. Likewise, trade in food and agricultural products doubled its share, while trade in fuels and minerals nearly lost half its value. Accounting for the particular impact the COVID-19 pandemic had on oil and gas global prices, was less abrupt and its dominance over trade in manufactured goods or agricultural products remained solid for most years. Nonetheless, the second decade of the century witnessed a significant increase on the share of these goods against fuels and minerals. In 2020, trade in manufactured goods and agricultural products amounted for 70% of the region's internal trade, while trade in agricultural products did essentially remain unaffected by the pandemic.

Figure 1.5. Evolution of trade in MENA countries by main commodity categories

% of total trade

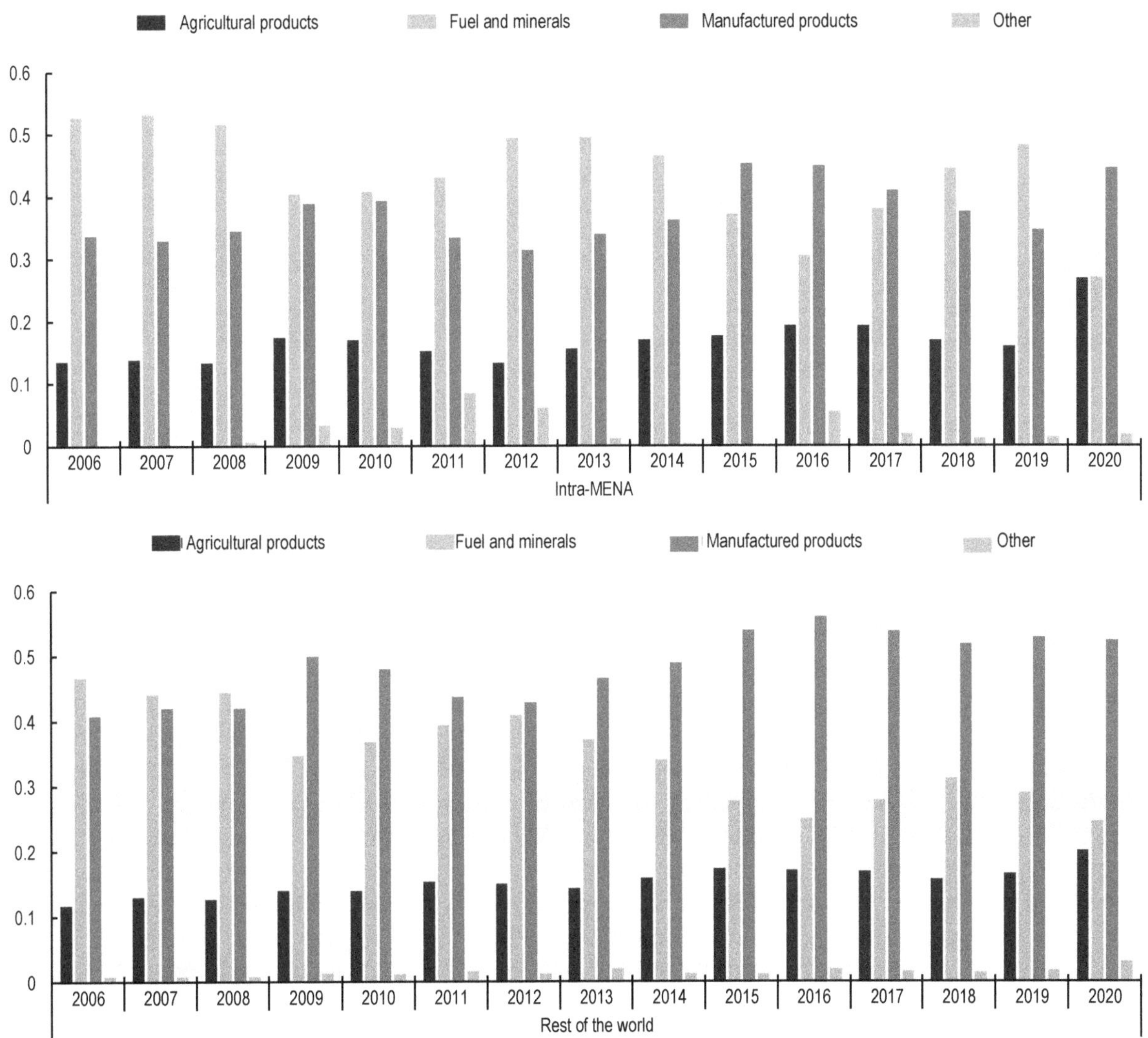

Note: Algeria's data for 2018, 2019 and Algeria's and Tunisia's data for 2020 is mirrored data from other reporting countries.
Source: OECD calculations, UN Comtrade database.

The global pandemic slowed down international trade in 2020, but trade gradually resumed in 2021. The MENA countries ultimately experienced less severe drops in trade flows in 2020 than initially estimated (Table 1.2).

Table 1.2. MENA and EU-27 total exports and imports, 2018-20

% of GDP

	Exports of goods and services			Imports of goods and services		
	2018	2019	2020	2018	2019	2020
Algeria	25.9	22.7	18.0	32.2	29.1	27.8
Egypt	18.9	17.5	13.1	29.4	25.7	20.7
Jordan	35.2	36.3	23.7	53.4	49.4	41.7
Lebanon	20.6	20.4	19.7	47.2	40.7	25.9
Mauritania	34.3	39.2	39.8	47.9	50.0	51.3
Morocco	38.8	39.3	34.9	49.2	47.9	42.6
Tunisia	45.7	40.9	32.9	58.6	52.9	39.6
Palestinian Authority	16.0	15.5	16.0	55.4	53.5	51.1
European Union	49.2	49.3	46.6	45.3	45.9	42.9

Note: Tunisia's exports and imports for 2019 and 2020 do not include services.
Source: World Bank national accounts data and OECD National Accounts data files.

Recent research on the impact of the pandemic suggested that trade subject to regional trade agreements (RTAs) was more resilient to the downturn: the decline for an average country was about - 13.8%, -14.1% without an RTA, -11.2 with an RTA and -8.5% if the RTA is deeply integrative (UNCTAD, 2021[30]). This holds for most RTAs involving MENA countries (Table 1.3), with differences depending on the direction of trade flows (export or import) and specific RTA agreement.

In particular, exports between MENA members of RTAs saw in 2020 a smaller drop, compared to 2019, than the countries' global export performance. Exports between signatory countries of the Agadir Trade agreement fell 4% in 2020, a significantly smaller contraction compared to the 9.8% drop Agadir countries experienced with their exports to the entire world. However, imports between Agadir signatory countries showed a bigger drop (38%) than that of their imports at the global level (13.83%), and a similar effect is observed among PAFTA/GAFTA adherents. This can be partially explained by the nature of the region's imports. For instance, Egypt's imports basket in 2020 was dominated by machinery (20% of the total imported products), cereals and other food products (13%), which mostly originate outside the MENA region, and are thus not covered by Agadir's or PAFTA/GAFTA's RTAs. On the other side, oil, a crucial commodity produced within the region, and reflected in PAFTA/GAFTA trade flows, suffered the biggest drop in value among all imported products in 2020 with respect to 2019 in countries like Jordan (-75%), Tunisia (-50%), Egypt (-45%), Lebanon (-36%) or Morocco (-32%).

In the context of the EU Association Agreements on Trade, in most cases, both exports and imports between the EU and MENA countries showed higher resilience in 2020 than overall trade in each respective country, with few exceptions, e.g. Egypt's and the Palestinian Authority's imports performed better globally than within their respective EU Association Agreements, and Jordan's exports to the EU were more disrupted in 2020 than the country's total exports.

From a policy perspective, to build resilience it is important to consider the nature of the trade interaction between partner countries (i.e. what is traded and the level of integration in GVCs), as well as the depth of trade agreements, which help explain the performance of trade in the case of global and regional shocks.

Table 1.3. Trade Agreements of MENA countries and trade changes, 2019-20

Billion, current USD; percentage

Agreement	Relation	Exports of goods		Imports of goods	
		2020	2020- 2019 change	2020	2020- 2019 change
Agadir Agreement	*Intra*	3.38	-4%	2.18	-39%
	Total	89.2	-9.8%	155.2	-14%
PAFTA/GAFTA	*Intra*	83.8	-7.71%	57.3	-27%
	Total	341	-16%	535	-19.6%
EU Association Agreements:					
Algeria	*Intra*	10.8	-30.59%	14.5	-20.77%
	Total	18.8	-42.51%	16.8	-22.22%
Egypt	*Intra*	9.66	-0.21%	19.56	-11.08%
	Total	33.6	-11.58%	56.84	-9.92%
Jordan	*Intra*	0.52	-4.68%	3.67	-14.05%
	Total	9.72	-9.79%	19.1	-16.96%
Lebanon	*Intra*	0.489	-4.68%	4.7	-31.99%
	Total	4.24	-9.79%	12.9	-32.81%
Morocco	*Intra*	19.95	-6.71%	23.5	-11.69%
	Total	32.2	-6.94%	43.2	-13.43%
Palestinian Authority	*Intra*	0.019	34.51%	0.48	-16.46%
	Total	1.15	-0.86%	5.42	-2.87%
Tunisia	*Intra*	10.63	-16.17%	10	-18.79%
	Total	13.7	-19.88%	16.5	-25.34%

Note: Intra refers to trade between the members of the RTA. Total refers to the total trade volume of the reporting country on a given year. PAFTA/GAFTA exports do not include exports to unspecified regions.
Source: OECD calculations, UN Comtrade database.

The trade agreements above portrayed reflect the Euro-Mediterranean countries efforts to reduce tariffs on trade of agricultural and manufactured goods, typically not covering trade in services. This contributes to the region's trade in goods dominance over a much more timid trade in services, which by nature require more ambitious agreements, which comprises consensus on multiple policy areas that have effects beyond the economic relations of signatory countries (OECD, 2021[12])[4].

MENA exported products that experienced the deepest impact were those more integrated in the global economy (based on 2020 Economic Complexity Index), notably fuel, for which a drop of 45% (more than USD 19 billion) was observed with respect to the 2019 levels, machinery (drop of 44%), electric machinery (42%), textiles, clothing and footwear (36%) and transport equipiment (21%). Exports of pharmaceutical products were relatively resilient, decreasing by less than 10%. Other resilient export products included ores, minerales and metals, chemicals and agricultural products (Figure 1.6).

Figure 1.6. MENA exports by sector, 2019-20

Billion, current USD

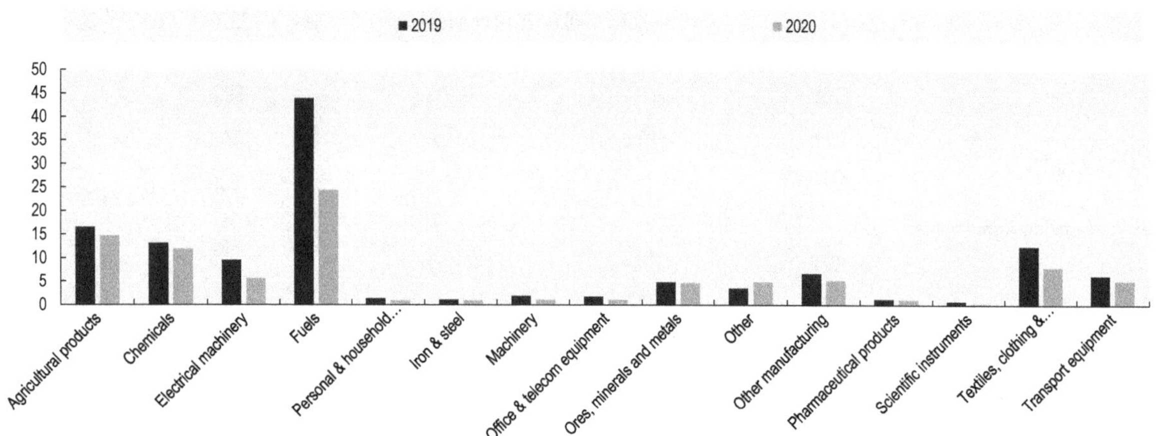

Source: OECD calculations, UN Comtrade database.

As was the case in other regions of the world, the contraction of trade in MENA stressed the importance of addressing structural problems, to boost trade competitiveness and at the same time strengthen economic resilience against crises.

Supply chains: Following the pandemic, the question of disruptions of supply chains has, indeed, become central in the policy debate on global trade. OECD estimates indicate that the extent of disruption to supply chains around the world was very heterogeneous - on average 7% in value terms over the course of 2020 (Arriola, Kowalski and van Tongeren, 2021[31]). Related to the analysis of the extent of disruptions, the COVID-19 crisis prompted work on ways to strengthen resilience of supply chains, with new tools being developed to guide both governments and businesses to better prepare to face different risks (see below under Policy considerations, the OECD's *4 keys to resilient supply chains*).

Trade in services: Even prior to the world pandemic, trade in services lagged behind trade in goods in MENA countries, except for Lebanon (Figure 1.7). This is due to the high degree of regulatory restrictiveness in the different countries, in the absence of international treaties liberalising services. Although less important than trade in goods, trade in services has a relevant place in the MENA countries. The average contribution of trade in services to GDP is higher in most MENA countries than the world average of 13.4%. Moreover, some economies are close to the figures found for the EU-27, the world's largest exporter and importer of services. On average, trade with the EU constitutes 26.3% of the total trade in services of the MENA countries, although with significant cross-country differences; specifically: 64.9% for Tunisia, 43.2% for Morocco, 36.5% forAlgeria, 30.6% for Egypt, 14.9% forJordan, 10% for Lebanon and 9.3% for the Palestinian Authority (EUROMESCO, 2021[32]), (European Union, 2021[33]).

Figure 1.7. Trade in services and goods, MENA countries and EU-27, 2017-20

As a % of GDP

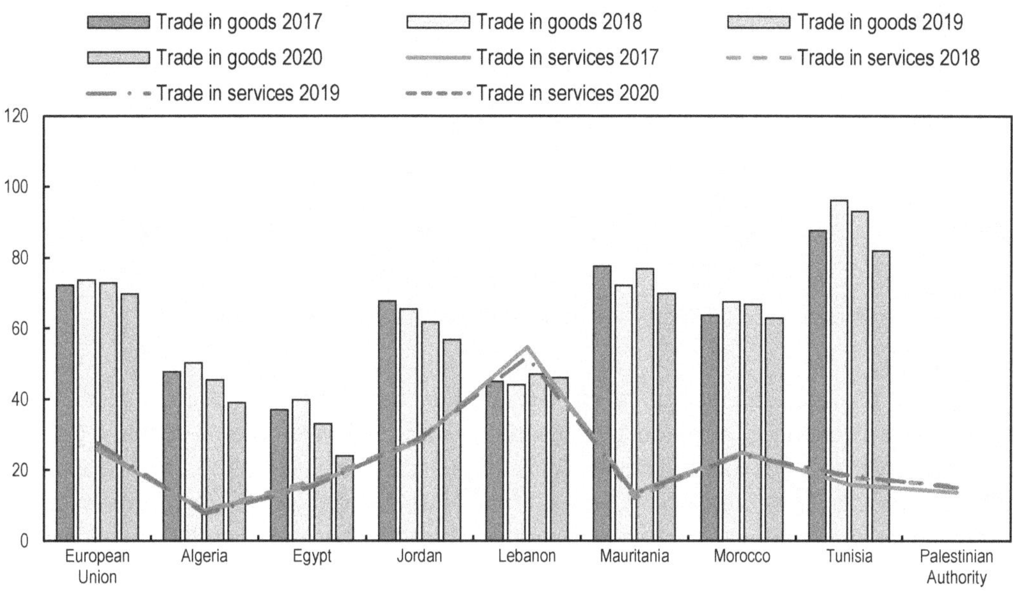

Note: Trade in goods as a share of GDP is the sum of merchandise exports and imports divided by the value of GDP, all in current USD; Trade in services is the sum of service exports and imports divided by the value of GDP, all in current USD.
Source: International Monetary Fund, Balance of Payments Statistics Yearbook and data files, and World Bank and OECD GDP estimates., https://data.worldbank.org/indicator/BG.GSR.NFSV.GD.ZS

Still, tradable and non-tradable services generate around half of the GDP of MENA countries, employing large shares of the labour force including in the public sector (OECD, 2021[12])(Figure 1.8) (Table 1.4).

Figure 1.8. Services, value added, MENA and EU-27, 2017-20

as % of GDP

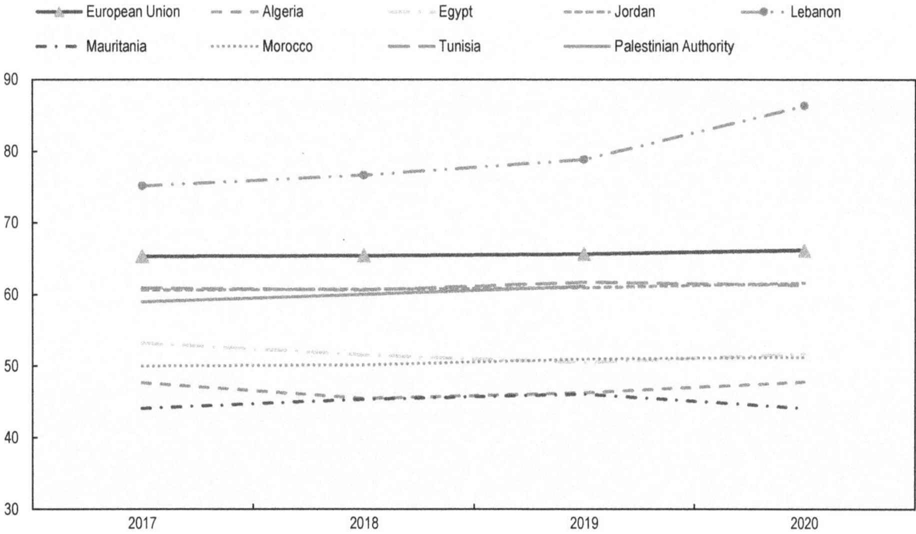

Source: World Bank national accounts data, and OECD National Accounts data files, https://data.worldbank.org/indicator/NV.SRV.TOTL.ZS

Table 1.4. Employment in services, 2020

% of total employment

	% of total employment	female (% of female employment)	male (% of male employment)
Algeria	59.99	73.13	57.52
Egypt	52.44	70.78	47.61
Jordan	73.09	86.27	70.46
Lebanon	65.1	77.59	61.25
Mauritania	51.56	60.63	47.47
Morocco	43.66	34.58	46.49
Palestinian Authority	63.59	85.6	59.48
Tunisia	52.75	58.47	50.94

Source: International Labour Organization, ILOSTAT database, Modeled ILO estimate, https://ilostat.ilo.org/data/?#

The importance of the services sector is related to the "servicification" of manufacturing, i.e the manufacturing sector increasingly relies on services that are bundled with material goods, e.g. installation, maintenance and repair services. Manufacturing firms more and more export services bundled with goods, and, through this process, firms create more value (Miroudot and Cadestin, 2017[34]). Moreover, evidence suggests that with servicification, service sectors with high productivity stimulate the productivity of other sectors, notably agriculture and manufacturing.

Most MENA countries are largely dependent on services sectors, but these sectors are underperforming. The value-added of services per worker ranges from USD 6 377 in Mauritania to USD 19 900 in Lebanon. These figures are in contrast to the high values found in Europe and OECD countries, respectively. This is due to the dependence on low productivity service sectors in the region, which are characterised by intensive face-to-face interactions, are less knowledge-intensive and employ a low-skilled workforce. This category includes transport, trade, travel and restaurant services (OECD, 2021[12]). Low-value-added services have been strongly disrupted by the containment measures. In contrast, high-productivity services sectors such as ICT, professional and financial services, were found to be resilient worldwide.

The recovery could provide the momentum in the broad MENA region for advancing the formalisation of international trade partnerships that facilitate trade in services. Such partnerships could in turn stimulate the development of high productivity services sectors through capacity building, infrastructure improvement, provision of capital, transfer of technology and know-how, and human capital development.

Trade facilitation: The performance of MENA countries on trade facilitation improved in recent years, but weaknesses remain in several areas (Figure 1.9) that should be addressed to enable trade expansion and sustain economic recovery. Figure 1.10 illustrates trade facilitation by country.

Figure 1.9. Trade facilitation, average MENA region, 2019

From 0 to 2 (best score)

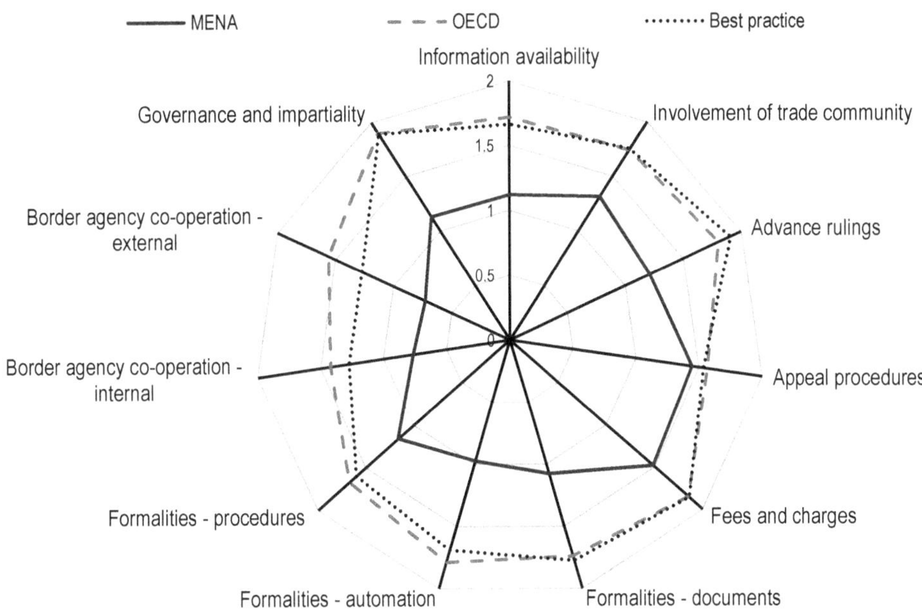

Note: Best practice represents the top 25% of countries covered by the OECD TFI indices average. Data are not available for the following UfM members of the MENA region: Mauritania and the Palestinian Authority.
Source: OECD Trade Facilitation Indicators (database), www.oecd.org/trade/facilitation/indicators.htm.

Figure 1.10. Trade facilitation in MENA countries, 2019

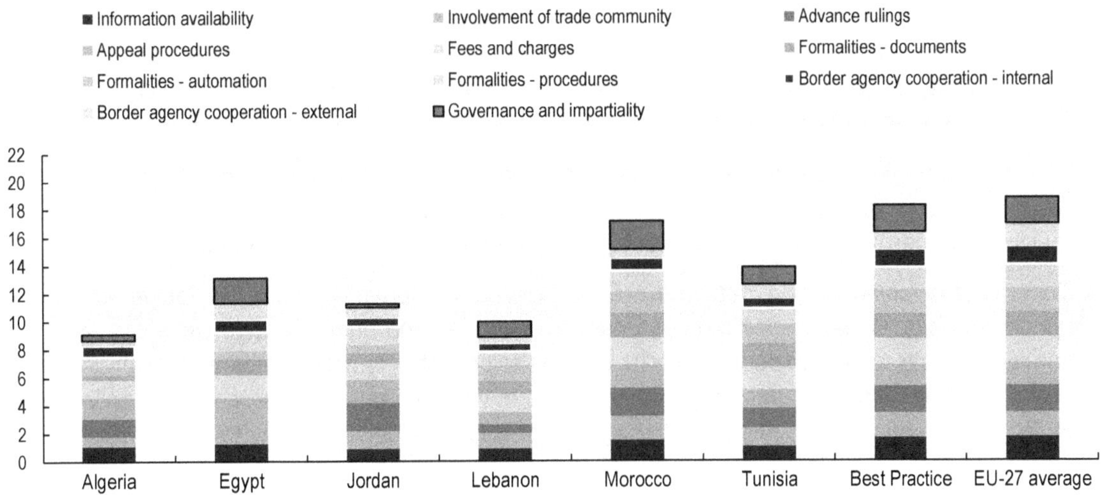

Note: Each single item has a score from 0 to 2 (best score). Best practice represents top 25% TFI performers average. Data are not available for the following UfM members of the MENA region: Mauritania and the Palestinian Authority.
Source: OECD Trade Facilitation Indicators database, http://www.oecd.org/trade/facilitation/indicators.htm.

Policy considerations

Two reflections should orient policy in support of trade in MENA countries post-pandemic. *First*, the pandemic confirmed the need to pursue a reform agenda to unleash the untapped trade potential in MENA countries, also in line with the recommendations of the 11th UfM Trade Ministerial Conference in November 2020 (UfM, 2020[35]). These involve:

- *Increase collaboration on trade regulations and agreements*, including the adoption and implementation of treaties that foster trade in services.
- *Enhance border cooperation with neighbouring countries and advance the automation of trade formalities to further reduce existing trade costs.* The minimisation of trade burdens could be achieved through the digitalisation of cross-border systems, custom patrols, entry points and the establishment of electronic single window systems for the registration of trade transactions.
- *Further invest in telecommunications and transport infrastructure.* MENA countries will need to improve their telecommunications infrastructure, a main barrier to high productivity sectors, especially in services. Improved transport infrastructure is equally critical for reducing the costs of trade in goods and encourage business expansions. Currently, the long time and high transport costs in trade with neighbouring countries in the broad MENA region can be dissuasive for businesses that envisage starting or expanding their exporting activities. Better transport infrastructure also allows businesses in rural and remote areas to connect to national and international production networks.
- *Support trade diversification.* The untapped trade potential, in particular South-South, is also a consequence of a limited or inadequate product offer. Improving the general environment for trade, including access to transport and finance, could therefore remain relatively ineffective in the absence of industrial diversification. MENA countries should continue to encourage and facilitate industrial diversification.
- *Improve production efficiency, technological capacity as well as technical and managerial skills* in order to catch up with the trends and opportunities in the use of technology. Moreover, expanding export activities to include non-traditional goods can have further positive impacts on the region's overall productivity.
- *Develop sound data and statistics for informing the design of effective trade policies and monitoring their implementation and impact.* Today, most MENA countries lack the data needed to assess their capacity to leverage the megatrends of globalisation and digitalisation to improve their international competitiveness.

Second, the crisis stressed the vulnerabilities associated with enhanced industrial and trade integration at a global and regional level, notably in sectors that provide essential goods and services, such as food, medical devices or energy. To increase resilience, measures to be considered include:

- *Enhance the collaboration between the public and the private sector, to tackle and prevent upcoming risks.* Collaboration between public authorities and businesses towards preventing and minimising risks and unexpected threats against supply chains can involve a clear understanding of the local and international actors participating in value chains and trade routes, collecting and sharing information, or developing stress tests for essential goods. Policy that seek strengthening the resilience of supply chains should also explore how to accompany the benefits from specialisation of existing industries with increased competition and diversification.
- *Implement national and regional mechanisms on resilient supply chains.* It is recommended to MENA countries to consider holistic policy tools, such as the OECD's *4 keys to resilient supply chains.* This has been developed as an interactive web tool, with the goals to deepen the common evidence base, identify a toolkit of options, and improve communication about the importance of

open markets during the pandemic. The tool is meant to help governments and businesses to address disruptions in international trade.

References

Arriola, C., P. Kowalski and F. van Tongeren (2021), "The impact of COVID-19 on directions and structure of international trade", *OECD Trade Policy Papers*, No. 252, OECD Publishing, Paris, https://doi.org/10.1787/0b8eaafe-en. [31]

Barry, S. (2021), *euronews.travel*, euronews.travel, https://www.euronews.com/travel/2021/05/26/travel-industry-experts-on-the-post-covid-travel-trends-emerging-from-bookings. [28]

C. Michael Hall, A. (2019), *Tourism and Innovation*, Routledge, https://doi.org/10.4324/9781315162836. [26]

Central Bank of Jordan (2020), *The Central Bank of Jordan announces a set of procedures aimed to contain the repercussions of the emerging Corona virus impact on the national economy*, https://www.cbj.gov.jo/DetailsPage/CBJEN/NewsDetails.aspx?ID=279. [20]

EC (2021), *Communication from the Commission to the European Parliament, the Council, the European Economic and Social Committee and the Committee of the Regions- Trade Policy Review - An Open, Sustainable and Assertive Trade Policy*, https://trade.ec.europa.eu/doclib/docs/2021/february/tradoc_159438.pdf. [36]

Egyptian Cabinet IDSC (2020), *Information and Decision Support Center*, https://www.idsc.gov.eg/. [24]

EUROMESCO (2021), *Post-COVID-19 EU-Sounthern Neighbourhood Trade Relations*, https://www.euromesco.net/wp-content/uploads/2021/05/Post-Covid-19-EU-SN-Trade-Relations.pdf. [32]

European Union (2021), *Trade - Countries and Regions*, https://ec.europa.eu/trade/policy/countries-and-regions/countries/. [33]

European Union (2020), *Digitalisation of Small and Medium Enterprises (SMEs) in the Mediterranean*, https://www.iemed.org/publication/digitalisation-of-small-and-medium-enterprises-smes-in-the-mediterranean/. [21]

IFC (2021), *How Firms Are Responding And Adapting During COVID-19 And Recovery*, https://www.ifc.org/wps/wcm/connect/publications_ext_content/ifc_external_publication_site/publications_listing_page/how+firms+are+responding+and+adapting+during+covid-19+and+recovery. [14]

IFC (2021), *IFC Knowledge Series in MENA - Overcoming Constraints to SME Development*, https://www.ifc.org/wps/wcm/connect/c458e2c5-1d69-40a5-8a85-9342f8d0fdb8/SME+Banking+in+MENA+-+issue+1.pdf?MOD=AJPERES&CVID=kcA9gOF. [11]

ILO (2021), *The impact of COVID-19 on enterprises in Jordan: One year into the pandemic*, https://www.ilo.org/beirut/media-centre/news/WCMS_814253/lang--en/index.htm. [9]

IMF (2021), *Policy responses to COVID-19*, https://www.imf.org/en/Topics/imf-and-covid19/Policy-Responses-to-COVID-19. [19]

IMF (2019), *Enhancing the role of SMEs in the Arab World*, https://www.imf.org/en/Publications/Policy-Papers/Issues/2019/12/13/Enhancing-the-Role-of-SMEs-in-the-Arab-World-Some-Key-Considerations-48873. [8]

MAGNiTT (2021), *MENA Q3 2021 Venture Investment Report*, https://magnitt.com/research/mena-q3-2021-venture-investment-report-50778. [17]

Miroudot, S. and C. Cadestin (2017), "Services In Global Value Chains: From Inputs to Value-Creating Activities", *OECD Trade Policy Papers*, No. 197, OECD Publishing, Paris, https://doi.org/10.1787/465f0d8b-en. [34]

OECD (2021), "An in-depth analysis of one year of SME and entrepreneurship policy responses to COVID-19: Lessons learned for the path to recovery", *OECD SME and Entrepreneurship Papers*, Vol. No. 25, https://doi.org/10.1787/6407deee-en. [10]

OECD (2021), "Issue Paper Session 4. Social resilience: moving away from informality to formal employment and businesses", *MENA-OECD Government Business Summit*, https://www.oecd.org/mena/competitiveness/issue-paper-session-4.pdf. [4]

OECD (2021), *Regional Integration in the Union for the Mediterranean: Progress Report*, OECD Publishing, Paris, https://doi.org/10.1787/325884b3-en. [12]

OECD (2021), *Social resilience: moving away from informality to formal*, https://www.oecd.org/mena/competitiveness/issue-paper-session-4.pdf. [7]

OECD (2020), *COVID-19 crisis in the MENA region: impact on gender equality and policy responses*, https://read.oecd-ilibrary.org/view/?ref=134_134470-w95kmv8khl&title=COVID-19-crisis-in-the-MENA-region-impact-on-gender-equality-and-policy-responses. [13]

OECD (2020), "Mitigating the impact of COVID-19 on tourism and supporting recovery", *OECD Tourism Papers*, No. 2020/03, OECD Publishing, Paris, https://doi.org/10.1787/47045bae-en. [25]

OECD (2020), *OECD Policy Responses to Coronavirus (COVID-19) : COVID-19 crisis in MENA countries*, https://www.oecd.org/coronavirus/policy-responses/covid-19-crisis-response-in-mena-countries-4b366396/. [2]

OECD (2020), *OECD Policy Responses to Coronavirus (COVID-19) : COVID-19 crisis in the MENA region: impact on gender equality and policy responses*, https://www.oecd.org/coronavirus/policy-responses/covid-19-crisis-in-the-mena-region-impact-on-gender-equality-and-policy-responses-ee4cd4f4/. [6]

OECD (2020), "Safe and seamless travel and improved traveller experience: OECD Report to G20 Tourism Working Group", *OECD Tourism Papers*, Vol. 2020/02, https://www.oecd-ilibrary.org/industry-and-services/safe-and-seamless-travel-and-improved-traveller-experience_d717feea-en. [29]

OECD/ILO/CAWTAR (2020), *Changing Laws and Breaking Barriers for Women's Economic Empowerment in Egypt, Jordan, Morocco and Tunisia*, Competitiveness and Private Sector Development, OECD Publishing, Paris, https://doi.org/10.1787/ac780735-en. [15]

Southan, J. (2021), *Travel-industry experts weigh-in on post-COVID trends*, https://www.euronews.com/travel/2021/05/14/what-will-travel-look-like-in-a-post-covid-world. [27]

UfM (2020), *Joint statement of the 11th Union for the Mediterranean (UfM) Trade Ministers Conference (10th November 2020)*, https://trade.ec.europa.eu/doclib/docs/2020/november/tradoc_159033.pdf. [35]

UNCTAD (2021), *Trade Agreements and Trade Resilience During COVID-19 Pandemic*, https://unctad.org/system/files/official-document/ser-rp-2021d13_en.pdf. [30]

UNWTO (2020), *The impact of COVID-19 on international tourism*, https://www.unwto.org/events/impact-of-covid-19-on-international-tourism. [22]

WAMDA (2021), "Startup Investment in MENA August 2021", https://www.wamda.com/2021/09/mena-startups-raised-160-million-august-2021. [18]

World Bank (2021), *Living with Debt : How Institutions Can Chart a Path to Recovery in the Middle East and North Africa*, https://openknowledge.worldbank.org/bitstream/handle/10986/35275/9781464816994.pdf. [16]

World Bank (2021), *MENA Development Report: Distributinal Impacts of COVID-19 in the Middle East and North Africa Region*, https://openknowledge.worldbank.org/bitstream/handle/10986/36618/9781464817762.pdf?sequence=2&isAllowed=y#page=58&zoom=100,188,761. [5]

World Bank (2021), *The Long Shadow of Informality*. [3]

World Bank (2021), *Worldwide Bureaucracy Indicators (WWBI)*, https://databank.worldbank.org/source/worldwide-bureaucracy-indicators-(wwbi). [1]

WTTC (2021), "Economic Impact Reports", *Economic Impact Reports*, https://wttc.org/Research/Economic-Impact (accessed on October 2021). [23]

Notes

[1] MENA region or MENA countries refer to the group of countries that are members of the Union for the Mediterranean. These countries are: Algeria, Egypt, Jordan, Lebanon, Mauritania, Morocco, Palestinian Authority and Tunisia. Where the term "broad MENA region" is used, it refers to the group of MENA countries that include UfM and non-UfM members.

[2] ILO Rapid Labour Force Surveys on the Impact of COVID-19, conducted in 2020 and 2021.

[3] Also, the Tunisian law n°38 of 2020 (not yet enforced) aims to recruit into the public sector unemployed graduates who have been unemployed for 10 years or more.

[4] Negotiations to create Deep and Comprehensive Free Trade Areas (DCFTAs) have been launched between the EU, Morocco, and Tunisia. In 2021, as part of the new EU trade policy review, the EU announced a sustainable investment initiative for interested partners in the Southern Neighbourhood and Africa (EC, 2021[36]).

2 Higher education and research

The COVID-19 crisis highlighted the central role of R&D in providing technical and scientific solutions to mitigate the negative effects of global shocks such as a pandemic. This chapter draws attention to the strategic importance of co-operation in research and innovation in the MENA region to help address common challenges, such as promoting the diversification of economic activities and fighting the effects of climate change.

Key takeaways

- The pandemic highlighted the central role of R&D in providing technical and scientific solutions in key areas to mitigate the negative effects of COVID-19. The drive for international scientific co-operation to find a cure for the virus could give momentum to increased political support for deepening co-operation at the regional level. Co-operation in research and innovation can help address common challenges in the MENA region, such as developing joint teaching and research funding programmes for collaborative research and skill development as well as promoting the diversification of economic activities.
- Maintaining R&D funding levels is a challenge for many countries in times of crisis. The current situation, however, does not seem to follow the same trend. Where previous crises have reduced R&D activity evenly, the COVID-19 crisis has created demand and investment in digital tools and digital health services. In some cases, it has also led to a re-allocation of public research and innovation funding to health and climate priorities and has accelerated trends already underway in STI. It has further opened access to data and publications, increased the use of digital tools, enhanced international collaboration, spurred a variety of public-private partnerships, and encouraged the active engagement of new players. These developments could speed the transition to a more open science and innovation in the longer run (OECD, 2021[1]).
- Moreover, investment in business R&D appears to be on an upward curve worldwide, albeit unevenly across industries. If this trend continues, the COVID-19 crisis will be the first global economic crisis in which business R&D spending has not declined in aggregate terms (OECD, 2021[2]). MENA countries could benefit from this, as R&D investments generate a return of almost twice the amount invested.
- The COVID-19 crisis points to radical changes in the educational and financial models of higher education institutions. Whether institutions will try to revert to the norm of the past, as has happened after previous crises, or whether they are prepared to adopt some of the innovative practices they have put in place, as the shift to increased digitalisation in higher education, remains open. There is a momentum to consider how to reshape higher education for long-term resilience.
- The crisis has an impact on people's ability to finance studies. Moreover, the losses in learning because of the pandemic might translate, in the medium term, into losses of job opportunities and income.
- Restrictions to mobility during the pandemic have pushed Higher Education to integrate digital technology into everyday teaching, and this trend should be further encouraged. The collateral impact of digitalisation on students' 'new' mobility could create opportunities for more South-South integration in education and distance education opportunities.
- The pandemic has revealed the extent of the digital divide and the socio-cultural inequalities present in the region. A particular effort should therefore be made to quantify equity in higher education and to consider measures to promote access to education for populations far from urban centres or vulnerable groups. This can be achieved among others through accelerating the process of digitalisation in higher education, improving the access to digital technologies and providing the relevant training to teachers to use digital platforms.
- The crisis created opportunities in higher education that should be fostered; specifically, the rise of educational technology (EdTech) could create employment and cooperation opportunities in the region. The EdTech market represents a huge potential for the broad MENA region, since on a regional scale, EdTech for higher education is still very limited while booming worldwide.

The broad MENA region[1] boasts over 100 million students. By 2050, more than 270 million children, adolescents and youth (0-24 years) will live, study and work in the region (World Bank, 2021[3]). In 2030, this will be equivalent to about 25 million additional students, or a 23% increase in the youth population, which will require to be accommodated in the education systems (OECD, 2021[4]) and in the labour market. Yet, the latter is not prepared for this increase: youth unemployment (15-24 years) is the highest in the world. Before the pandemic, nearly 30% of adolescents and youth in North Africa, and just over 20% in the Arab states of the MENA region, were unemployed. For young women, the rate is even higher. The region's youth population was already living in fear of a difficult future; the health crisis has further disrupted access to learning opportunities and completely (or significantly) changed the paradigm of higher education in the region. Nonetheless, the economic recovery already underway has a tremendous potential to capitalise on innovative education, new technologies and to foster the growth of a generation of learners that has the prospective to transform the broad MENA region.

Cooperation in research on relevant industrial sectors and to address common challenges

COVID-19 created a shift in the global economy - in particular, the digital transformation has exponentially accelerated, transformed the balance of global production and is affecting the ability of countries to follow regional integration strategies based solely on trade and foreign investment policies. Promoting structural change in the region's economies through regional cooperation in higher education and science will be crucial to the countries' ability to seize opportunities in this changing global context. In that regard, co-operation in research can help address rampant questions in the MENA economies, such as improving the number and quality of skilled labour as well as promoting the diversification of economic activities. It can also help in providing solutions to shared regional problems such as political stability, energy, transport and telecommunications infrastructures, clean water, and sustainable agriculture (OECD, 2021[5]). Overall, R&D policies should be seen as accompanying the integration of economies at the regional level:

- Strong links between research, education and industry at the national level play an important role in attracting higher value-added foreign investment from multinational companies and in enabling international cooperation (World Bank, 2020[6]).

The central role of **R&D in providing technical and scientific solutions in key areas to mitigate the negative effects of the COVID-19 pandemic could give momentum to increased political support for research** and address the need for regional co-operation. This could lead to a significant increase in public investment in universities and public research institutions. Health-related research, in particular, could benefit from such investments, especially those aimed at preparing for future pandemics. Other sectors or technology areas (e.g. Industry 4.0, Artificial Intelligence [AI]) are seen as strategic for moderninizing manufacturing and services and improving preparedness for future shocks and challenges, such as climate change. Especially as research in key areas is recognised as fundamental to achieving sustainable economic growth and addressing some of the biggest challenges to achieving the Sustainable Development Goals (SDGs) (Borowiecki et al., 2019[7]). Under the 2030 Agenda of the SDGs, countries have committed to "build resilient infrastructure, promote inclusive and sustainable industrialisation and foster innovation". In particular, SDG 9.5 calls on them to "encourage innovation and substantially increase the number of researchers, as well as public and private spending on research and experimental development". The best example to prove the link between a vibrant R&D and progress are the collaborative global initiatives to develop an effective vaccine and treatments for COVID-19 that emerged in 2020 and 2021. The impressive speed at which global companies developed vaccines was built on years of public research spending, existing global research infrastructures /networks and new technology platforms. But the unequal distribution of these benefits reminds us that national interests can undermine co-operation among countries. It also points to the need to build capacity for research and technology in middle income and developing countries and the role that multilateral actors (e.g. IGOs, MDBs, ODA) must play in boosting STI capabilities globally (OECD, 2021[1]).

On the co-operation side, regional integration in research and higher education requires pre-conditions at the national level (OECD, 2021[5]). Countries need to invest in their own national science and technology capacities in order to be able to absorb technologies resulting from co-operation with foreign structures.

In that regard, when examining regional results, while the proportion of global GDP invested in R&D has increased from 1.62% in 2010 to 1.72% in 2018, regions are increasingly heterogeneous in terms of spending. The broad MENA region spends less of its GDP on R&D than the worlds average and the 2.5% average of western economies (Western Europe and North America) (UNESCO Institute for Statistics, 2021[8]).

The number of researchers per million inhabitants also shows a large disparity in the world, following a similar pattern to that of the evolution of R&D expenditure. Indeed, a large part of R&D expenditure is allocated to researchers' salaries and wages. At the global level, the number of researchers per million inhabitants is 1,198 (in 2017). Europe and North America are above the world average with 3,707 researchers per million inhabitants, on average, whereas the broad MENA region revolves around 1,000, with a very notable counter example: Tunisia having 1,800 researchers per million inhabitants (Table 2.1)

Table 2.1. R&D in selected MENA countries

Country	R&D spending as of % of GDP	R&D spending in Purchasing Power Parity $	R&D spending by sector performance	Number of researchers per million inhabitants	% of male and female researchers
Algeria	0.6%	$ 2,595.7M	-	919	65% male 35% female
Egypt	0.7%	$6,271.1M	Business $503,583.2k Government $2,263.1M Universities $3,502.4M Private non-profit $1,984.4k	675	58% male 42% female
Jordan	0.4%	$265,567.1k	-	-	78% male 23% female
Morocco	0.7%	$1,485.1M	Business $444.616.8k Government $342,571.0k Universities $697,939.1k	1,024	68% male 32% female
Tunisia	0.7%	$756,067.2k	Business $139,872.8k Government $381,813.6k Universities $234,380,8k	1,814	46% male 54% female

Note: Data refer to the latest available year: 2018, 2017 or 2016. Data for Lebanon, Mauritania and Palestinian Authortiy are not available; R&D personnel in a statistical unit include all persons engaged directly in R&D, whether employed by the statistical unit or external contributors fully integrated into the statistical unit's R&D activities, as well as those providing direct services for the R&D activities (such as R&D managers, administrators, technicians and clerical staff).
Source: (UNESCO Institute for Statistics, 2021[9]), http://uis.unesco.org/apps/visualisations/research-and-development-spending/

It is therefore essential that MENA countries do not shift their fiscal support for research and development to other short-term stimulus projects, and that the former does not become the forgotten sector of the post-COVID-19 recovery (World Bank, 2020[6]).

The areas of research and higher education are not *prima facie* a direct focus of regional integration policies that aim to reduce divisions and market barriers to trade and exchange (OECD, 2021[5]). The increased levels of public debt across the world, could reduce funding for public universities and research institutions. The experience from the world's global financial crisis from 2008-09 showed that a decrease in R&D funding levels led to damages in countries' innovation capacities and exacerbated the risk of brain drain of researchers, including in MENA countries (OECD, 2021[10]). Recent developments in the dynamics of the COVID-19 crisis however tend to distance the current situation from the 2008 one (OECD, 2021[10]). Indeed, **the pandemic has created unprecedented demand in a number of R&D sectors, notably for digital tools and digital health services**, while other sectors (e.g. automotive, aerospace) have been hit hard, indicating a very heterogeneous dynamic between sectors, which was not the case in previous crises (Paunov and Planes-Satorra, 2021[11]).

Moreover, a preliminary indication of how business R&D in OECD fared during the COVID-19 crisis done by the OECD in Q1 2021 established that investment continued to grow in OECD member states in 2020, although at a significantly lower rate than in 2019 and with big differences across industries. Both the information and communications technology (ICT) and the life sciences industries fared well in 2020, less so in other industries such as transport equipment (OECD, 2021[12]). If further confirmed by official data , this would be the first global economic crisis in the OECD's 60-year history during which business R&D expenditures did not decline at the aggegate level; a reassuring trend that MENA countries could take advantage of, considering that studies have found that investments in R&D generate nearly twice the sum invested in return (UNESCO Institute for Statistics, 2021[8]).

Research in the broad MENA region is centred on the South-North axis. While maintaining this axis, the MENA countries could consider further regional integration, better suited to meet their specific needs. Currently, most scientific cooperation is organised around the physical sciences and chemistry as well as the life sciences, which are important areas for industrial development. Scientific cooperation in the field of environmental sciences is less strong in the UfM countries of the South, yet there is a growing demand for research collaboration in this field. Especially considering the potential regional impact of climate change on the region's water, food and agricultural systems. Participation in international research collaboration can take many forms, from bilateral programmes to international collaborative programmes. In addition to sharing costs and improving the quality of scientific research and training, international research programmes are also a means of directing research towards common problems (OECD, 2021[5]).

Policy considerations

In order to further promote cooperation in research on relevant industrial sectors and address common challenges, the MENA countries could take the following policy considerations into account, building on UfM's Renewed strategic agenda for higher education and regional cooperation in the Mediterranean (UfM, 2019[13]):

- *Further tailor research to the regions' specific needs through cooperation*, in order to find solutions to shared regional problems. Especially, in the field of environmental sciences, there is a growing demand for research foreseen due to the impacts climate change has had on the broad MENA region's water, food and agricultural systems. Moreover, research can help address other important questions, as improving the number and quality of skilled labour and promoting economic diversification.
- *Encourage further South-North integration in research*. Participation in international research collaborations enables countries to share costs, improve the quality of research and training, as well as effectively address common problems. However, the necessary pre-conditions at the national level have to be created by MENA countries. Countries need to invest in their own national science and technology capacities in order to be able to absorb technologies resulting from cooperation with foreign research institutions.
- *Ensure sustained R&D funding amid the post-COVID-19 recovery phase*. Former experiences, e.g. the 2008-09 financial crisis, have demonstrated that maintaining R&D spending is crucial to avoid damage to innovation capacities as well as risking brain drain of researchers.

Digital technology for higher education

COVID-19 has thrown millions of students into the new reality of distance learning. However, internet access, sufficient bandwidth and reliability are still a challenge for many countries in the broad MENA region. Compared with other regions, MENA has one of the lowest fixed-broadband subscription rates per 100 inhabitants, although this is partly explained by average household size (and composition), which is larger on average than in OECD member states. Internet use by the MENA population generally ranges between 59% and 79% with a notable exception in Mauritania (Figure 2.1).

Figure 2.1. Individuals using the Internet in the MENA region

% of population, latest available year

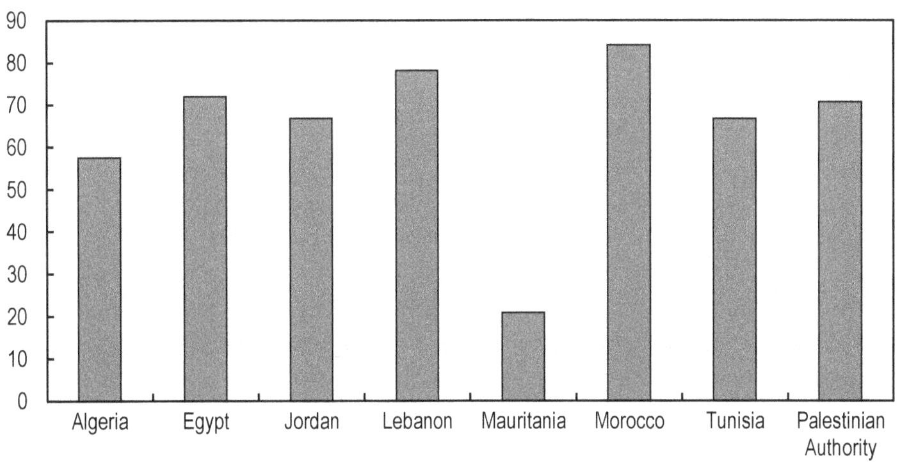

Note: Data refer to 2017 for Jordan, Lebanon and Mauritania; to 2019 for Algeria, Tunisia and the Palestinian Authority; to 2020 for Egypt and Morocco.
Source: World Bank, World Development Indicators, 2021, https://databank.worldbank.org/source/world-development-indicators.

Internet use is most often by mobile and much less by fixed-broadband. Indeed, none of the countries in the region, except for Tunisia, has more than 10 fixed-broadband subscriptions per 100 inhabitants, well below the figures for OECD countries and the EU-27 (Figure 2.2). The International Telecommunication Union (ITU) estimated a fixed-broadband penetration level of 8.1 subscriptions per 100 inhabitants for the region as a whole in 2020, about half of the global average of 15.2 subscriptions per 100 inhabitants.[2]

Conversely, the region's population is using mobile internet networks. Some countries, such as Morocco and Tunisia, have more mobile subscriptions than OECD countries. In countries where power cuts are frequent and the bandwidth low, online teaching and learning can be less effective. Frequent power outages have caused students in some UfM members to lose an average of up to 10 minutes per session, making learning a challenge (Jawabreh, 2020[14]).

Figure 2.2. Mobile cellular and fixed broadband subscriptions in the MENA region

2019 and 2020

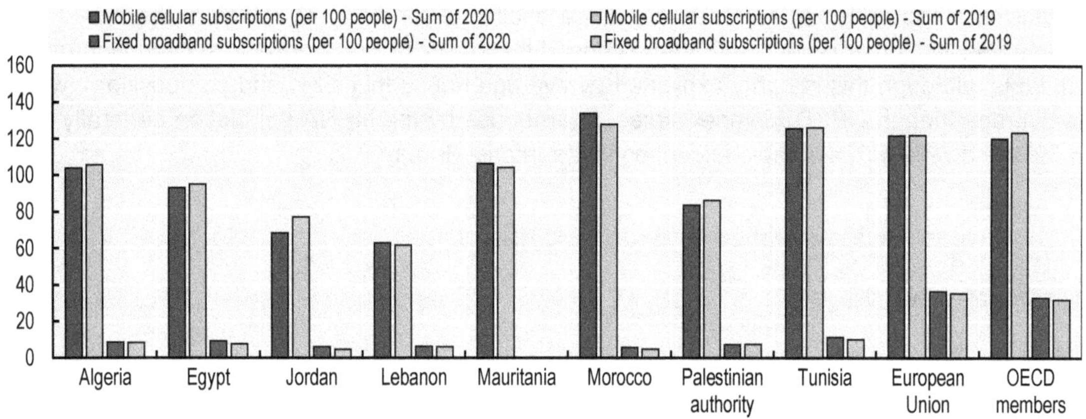

Source: WB, World Development Indicators, 2021, https://databank.worldbank.org/source/world-development-indicators.

At the height of the COVID-19 crisis, the inequalities mentioned above were echoed in disparities in higher education. Vulnerable populations and women, risk facing disproportionate difficulties in accessing ICT-based learning, due to their overall lower levels of digital inclusion and were more likely to be pushed out of university and training systems during COVID-19 (OECD, 2020[15]). Difficulties included among other limited hardware such as tablets and laptops for student use at home, students not having devices and only using their phones for online courses; and limited availability of online course content/ability to move classes online (e.g. lab work in medicine or chemistry). Further challenges were instructors' limited digital and pedagogical skills, for instance for online teaching and student assessment, and limited training in this area (World Bank, 2021[16]).

In general, the economic impacts of pandemics disproportionately affect women's drop-out rates in regions where the gender inequalities are pronounced (UNESCO, 2020[17]). A study on the Ebola outbreak in West Africa found that during the health crisis, girls whose mothers were infected were forced to take over their care-giving responsibilities (Care, 2020[18]), which may hinder their possibility of returning to school and university. Girls' educational outcomes in general may also suffer if girls are asked to contribute to household activities more than boys' at the expense of their home-based learning (OECD, 2020[15]).

COVID-19 has had a major impact on the population's ability to finance studies in MENA countries and universities financing is at stake. The pandemic and the ensuing economic crisis are likely to have a major impact on the education sector in the broad MENA region, including its financing by governments, private households and donors.

Governments may be forced to reduce investments in schools and universities to compensate for large public expenditures mainly in the health sector, although there are positive examples around the world of countries, albeit mostly in developed ones, that have recognised the importance of higher education in their stimulus packages. The United States of America, for instance, put in place a stimulus bill set to give nearly USD 170 billion to education, including USD 40 billion to higher education (United States, 2021[19]). This trend is not yet confirmed in the MENA region, however, prior to the global health crisis, MENA governments were investing heavily in higher education, at a level similar to the world average of 4.5% of GDP (World Bank, 2021[20]). Some countries even exceeded this average: Tunisia spent more than 20% of its national budget on education (6.6% of its GDP) (OECD, 2021[5]). Egypt has also largely increased its education (including higher education) spending in the last decade and continued through 2020 and 2021, with a 13% increase in allocations for education, higher education, health, and scientific research in its

2021 budget. The four sectors are supposed to receive a total of EGP 727.8 billion (EUR 40.2 billion) (Ministry of International Cooperation, 2020[21]).

Similarly, in many MENA countries for which data are available, per capita spending on higher education in relative terms tends to be higher than in industrialised countries. Even countries, such as Tunisia, that face financial constraints tend to spend more in relative terms than OECD countries (World Bank, 2021[22]). However, this trend is heterogeneous across the region, with countries such as Jordan and Mauritania spending less. It is also important to note that not all universities will be impacted in the same way. Private universities, which are numerous in the MENA region, are likely to be more exposed to the economic shock due to the decrease in received tuition fees (World Bank, 2021[3]). Reduced incomes will make it difficult for some families to cover the costs of education and for many MENA university students to finance their studies. This potential decrease in collected fees and scholarships could worsen the situation of universities. This could ultimately lead universities to hire less or even lay off staff, which would affect the quality of education provided. In addition, some of the region's private universities maintain their financial stability through private donations and sponsorships, often from wealthy families or foundations. The COVID-19 crisis might however have repercussions on financial capacity of donors and/or induce them to reconsider their donations.

COVID-19 may have substantially reduced the future earnings of students and young graduates in the broad MENA region. The OECD estimates that pandemic-induced learning discontinuity will translate into a 1.5% drop in GDP worldwide (OECD, 2021[4]). The learning losses of students affected by the COVID-19 pandemic will, in the medium term, translate into losses of experience, job opportunities and therefore income. Globally, the average student is expected to face a reduction of 2-8% in expected annual earnings.

The broad MENA region appears to be potentially in the high range in terms of annual income losses of students. The World Bank estimates that the losses per student per year, range from USD 457 to USD 1,789 (Azevedo et al., 2020[23]). This is significantly higher than estimates for other regions, such as South Asia (USD 116 to USD 319) or Latin America and the Caribbean (USD 242 to USD 835). For Jordanian students alone, the decline in average future annual income could be as high as 8%. Expressed in terms of the loss of present value of lifetime economic earnings (taking into account average adult survival and labour force participation rates) for all Jordanian students, the reductions due to COVID-19 could amount to USD 14 billion (World Bank, 2021[16]). Moreover, this estimate represents only the expected impact of learning losses and does not take into account the deteriorating prospects of youth employment post-COVID-19.

The pandemic has propelled schools to integrate digital technology into everyday teaching. Unlike many sectors that have undergone profound change due to the advancement of technology in recent decades, the education sector had largely maintained a brick-and-mortar infrastructure and face-to-face service. COVID-19 changed this paradigm. One change that is likely to remain after the end of the pandemic is the increased integration of digital technologies in higher education (OECD, 2020[24]). At the beginning of the crisis, a vast majority of universities were caught off guard by the containment measures, with a large proportion lacking the infrastructure and digital tools to deliver courses at a distance. Some of the first courses had to be delivered by improvised means, making extensive use of social networks and other computer messaging systems. After the initial shock, structured and effective teaching has been put in place in most of the MENA economies. Worldwide, the same shift towards technology is leading to what can be described as a real transition of higher education towards digitalisation whether in course design, teaching, evaluation or learning analysis and graduation (OECD, 2021[4]).

A year and a half into the crisis, there is an increased demand from students, and prospective students, for more flexible study options, including e-learning and part-time options. For instance, Egypt in partnership with Microsoft, launched its first digital platform on the website of the Ministry of Education to enable distance learning at the country's universities (Egypt, 2021[25]).[3]

Prior to COVID-19, distance education has been envisaged as a subsidiary means to traditional face-to-face teaching. In countries with universities with high logistical capacities, this mode of education was primarily designed to promote access to training for specific groups (e.g. continuing education, students with disabilities or living in remote areas). However, in countries such as India and China, distance learning has been used to reduce inequality in access to education and make it possible to enrol a larger proportion of the population in education overall, from primary to higher, for instance where the infrastructure of universities is thinner and sometime with insufficient intake capacity. The MENA region could possibly capitalise on both approaches (World Bank / CMI, 2021[26]).

The digitalisation of higher education and its impact on students' international mobility could eventually create opportunities for more integration of higher education in MENA. The COVID-19 pandemic has slowed down international mobility of students because of the temporary closures of borders and uncertainties about the near future concerning new closures and lockdowns. It is possible that MENA students will regard universities in nearer countries as more interesting options in the next years, provided that the quality of the university teaching and programmes are suitable.

Students in the broad MENA region tend to be more mobile than the world average. While 2.4% of students worldwide go abroad for their studies, this figure rises to 4.5% for MENA students. For example, in Mauritania 19.6% of students move abroad (UNESCO, 2021[27]), while in Jordan and Lebanon students who choose to go abroad are 8.3% and 7.8% (OECD, 2021[5]). Also, in these two countries, foreign students represent respectively 14.3% and 9% of total enrolment (on average in the years 2016-2019).

These figures are likely to change significantly in the post COVID-19 period. The pandemic has given rise to the concept of 'at home' mobility and has swept away the preconception of distance education as a stopgap measure. Indeed, distance learning has a strong potential for development. Opening up distance education provision to learners living beyond national borders would seem to be the best way to overcome not only the difficulties of the current context, but also the lack of access to education for people who do not have the opportunity to study abroad. It also represents an asset for the internationalisation of higher education institutions: as a showcase for the quality of the training offered, distance learning can be seen as an instrument for promotion abroad. In this sense, the MENA countries have the advantage of being able to boast a relative cultural and linguistic proximity, favouring South-South exchanges and mobility.

Until now, and unlike other regions in the world where institutions tend to give priority to other organisations in the same geographical sphere, most MENA institutions have preferred to develop partnerships with institutions outside the region. In the Maghreb, only the two trans-Mediterranean partnerships: the Franco-Tunisian University for Africa and the Mediterranean, and the Euro-Mediterranean University of Fez are exceptions (World Bank / CMI, 2021[26]).

The pandemic has created the potential for intra-regional or at least South-South cooperation in the internalisation of education. Several Egyptian universities, for example, are expanding their reach in Africa by broadening their offerings to promote higher education development and regional cooperation. For example, Ain Shams University in Cairo will build a branch in Dar el Salaam, Tanzania. An agreement to establish a branch of the Egyptian University of Tanta in Djibouti City has also been signed (World Bank, 2021[3]). Taking into account that for some countries, such as Morocco, Africa provides the largest pool of foreign students (UNESCO, 2021[27]), South-South integration is an opportunity to explore.

Investments in industry for educational technology (EdTech) have boomed and could create employment opportunities.

Knowledge generated by education and research institutions has the potential to help local firms move up the value chain and diversify production and access new markets (OECD, 2021[5]). The increased adoption of technology innovations in higher education and the rising demand for tools to personalise education have been accompanied by an increase in investment. According to a report by Global Ventures, the

EdTech sector - understood as the combined use of hardware, software and educational theory and practice to facilitate learning and its industry of companies that create educational technologies - entered the 2010s with USD 500 million in venture capital investments and finished 14 times higher with USD 7 billion in 2019 (Global Ventures, 2021[28]).

EdTech companies also attracted USD 8.3 billion in venture capital funding in the first three quarters of 2020 (Holon IQ, 2021[29]), of which USD 30 million were invested in the broad MENA region. This number may seem small compared to the total amount, but it is growing exponentially year-on-year. The Jordanian start-up, Abwaab, in particular, raised USD 2.4 million in 2019, a round touted as one of the largest pre-seed raised by a start-up in the region (Global Ventures, 2021[28]). Overall, the sector was valued at USD 250 billion in 2020 in the broad MENA region, and it could reach up to USD 404 billion by 2025. This would make it just over 5.4% of world's global education market of USD 7.3 trillion.

This market represents a huge business potential for the broad MENA region, since on a regional scale, the EdTech for higher education and continuous learning is still very limited, with most investment from start-ups focused on K-12 education (from kindergarten to 12th grade, i.e. 17-18 years old) and tutoring, which is a very common practice in the region (Holon IQ, 2021[30]).

Policy considerations

In order to decrease the digital divide and ensure equal access to education for all, MENA countries could take the following recommendations into consideration:

- *Reshape higher education for long-term resilience*. More innovative approaches to education and more resilient institutional business model. To this end, MENA countries could further invest in industry for educational technology, which is on the rise and has tremendous potential for transforming the education sector.
- *Accelerate digitalisation in higher education*. In order to reduce the digital divide and ensure education for all, countries need to ensure equal access to digital technologies in higher education. Moreover, in order to ensure a smooth transition to further use of digital technologies in higher education, trainings could be delivered to ensure that all teachers are able to use collaborative platforms (audio, video and web) correctly, and university teachers could be encouraged to obtain certifications in this field.
- *Further encourage South-South integration in education and distance education opportunities*. This enables universities in the MENA countries to expand their course offerings and for students to participate in short-distance learning courses. Moreover, it could give students who currently cannot go abroad, out of financial reasons or due to the pandemic, the opportunity to study at different regional institutions.
- *Promote the streamlining of university curricula with transitions into the labour market*. Prior to COVID-19, students stayed in education longer to better prepare themselves to enter a labour market that offered scarce opportunities. However, the COVID-19 crisis has changed this by limiting the financial capacity of the region's population to pursue longer studies. It is therefore essential to adapt the educational offer to the needs of the future labour market.

References

Azevedo, J. et al. (2020), *Simulating the Potential Impacts of COVID-19 School Closures on Schooling and Learning Outcomes: A Set of Global Estimates*, World Bank, Washington, DC, https://doi.org/10.1596/1813-9450-9284. [23]

Borowiecki, M. et al. (2019), "Supporting research for sustainable development", *OECD Science, Technology and Industry Policy Papers*, No. 78, OECD Publishing, Paris, https://doi.org/10.1787/6c9b7be4-en. [7]

Care (2020), *Gender analysis: Prevention and response to Ebola Virus Disease in the Democratic Republic of Congo*, https://reliefweb.int/report/democratic-republic-congo/gender-analysis-prevention-and-response-ebola-virus-disease. [18]

Egypt, M. (2021), *Unified Portal for Egyptian Universities*, https://egypt-hub.edu.eg/. [25]

Global Ventures (2021), *EdTech in the Middle East and Africa : An overview*, https://globalventures.docsend.com/view/69wenuk7vsvn4qy5. [28]

Holon IQ (2021), *Global EdTech Funding 2021 - Half Year Update : $10B of EdTech investment in 1H 2021 through 568 EdTech Funding Rounds*, https://www.holoniq.com/notes/global-edtech-funding-2021-half-year-update/. [29]

Holon IQ (2021), *MENA EdTech. Accelerating innovation across the Middle East and North Africa.*, https://www.holoniq.com/notes/mena-edtech-accelerating-innovation-across-the-middle-east-and-north-africa/. [30]

Jawabreh, A. (2020), "Gaza's University Students Drop Out at an Accelerating Rate Due to the Pandemic."", *Al-Fanar*, https://www.al-fanarmedia.org/2020/10/gaza-university-students-drop-out-at-an-accelerating-rate-due-to-the-pandemic/. [14]

Ministry of International Cooperation (2020), *COVID-19 Response & Rebuild*, https://drive.google.com/file/d/1a2IaAE6Jw38WwgaNSfoguthv29qYUaon/view. [21]

OECD (2021), *Main Science and Technology Indicators: Highlights March 2021*, https://www.oecd.org/sti/msti-highlights-march-2021.pdf. [2]

OECD (2021), *OECD Main Science and Technology Indicators Highlights on R&D expenditure, March 2021 release*, https://www.oecd.org/sti/msti-highlights-march-2021.pdf. [12]

OECD (2021), *OECD Policy Responses to Coronavirus (COVID-19) : How will COVID-19 reshape science, technology and innovation?*, https://www.oecd.org/coronavirus/policy-responses/how-will-covid-19-reshape-science-technology-and-innovation-2332334d/. [10]

OECD (2021), *OECD Science, Technology and Innovation Outlook 2021: Times of Crisis and Opportunity*, OECD Publishing, Paris, https://doi.org/10.1787/75f79015-en. [1]

OECD (2021), *Regional Integration in the Union for the Mediterranean: Progress Report*, OECD Publishing, Paris, https://doi.org/10.1787/325884b3-en. [5]

OECD (2021), *The State of Higher Education: One Year into the COVID-19 Pandemic*, OECD Publishing, Paris, https://doi.org/10.1787/83c41957-en. [4]

OECD (2020), *Digitalisation today: Benefits and risks for teaching and learning*, https://www.oecd.org/education/higher-education-policy/Digitalisation-today-webinar-key-messages.pdf. [24]

OECD (2020), *OECD Policy Responses to Coronavirus (COVID-19) : COVID-19 crisis in the MENA region: impact on gender equality and policy responses*, https://www.oecd.org/coronavirus/policy-responses/covid-19-crisis-in-the-mena-region-impact-on-gender-equality-and-policy-responses-ee4cd4f4/. [15]

Paunov, C. and S. Planes-Satorra (2021), "Science, technology and innovation in the time of COVID-19", *OECD Science, Technology and Industry Policy Papers*, No. 99, OECD Publishing, Paris, https://doi.org/10.1787/234a00e5-en. [11]

UfM (2019), *A renewed strategic agenda for higher education regional cooperation in the Mediterranean*, https://ufmsecretariat.org/higher-education-cairo-2019/. [13]

UNESCO (2021), *Global Flow of Tertiary-Level Students*, http://uis.unesco.org/en/uis-student-flow. [27]

UNESCO (2020), *Covid-19 school closures around the world will hit girls hardest*, https://read.oecd-ilibrary.org/view/?ref=134_134470-w95kmv8khl&title=COVID-19-crisis-in-the-MENA-region-impact-on-gender-equality-and-policy-responses. [17]

UNESCO Institute for Statistics (2021), *Global Investments in R&D Fact Sheet No. 59 June 2020*, http://uis.unesco.org/sites/default/files/documents/fs59-global-investments-rd-2020-en.pdf. [8]

UNESCO Institute for Statistics (2021), *How much your country invest in R&D*, http://uis.unesco.org/apps/visualisations/research-and-development-spending/. [9]

United States (2021), *American Rescue Plan 2021*, https://www.whitehouse.gov/american-rescue-plan/. [19]

World Bank (2021), *COVID-19 Coronavirus Response: Middle East and North Africa: Tertiary education*, https://thedocs.worldbank.org/en/doc/401131613571399876-0090022021/original/MENATEandCovidupdated.pdf. [3]

World Bank (2021), *Education Expenditure, Enrolment Dynamics and the Impact of COVID-19 on Learning in Jordan*, Washington, D.C. : World Bank Group., http://documents.worldbank.org/curated/en/410761619642824370/Education-Expenditure-Enrolment-Dynamics-and-the-Impact-of-COVID-19-on-Learning-in-Jordan. [16]

World Bank (2021), *Government expenditure on education, total (% of GDP) - Algeria, Jordan, Egypt, Lebanon, Mauritania, Morocco, Tunisia, West Bank and Gaza, OECD members*, https://data.worldbank.org/indicator/SE.XPD.TOTL.GD.ZS?locations=DZ-JO-EG-LB-MR-MA-TN-PS-OE. [22]

World Bank (2021), *World Development Indicators*, https://databank.worldbank.org/source/education-statistics-%5E-all-indicators. [20]

World Bank (2020), *Trading together: Reviving Middle East and North Africa Regional Integration in the Post Covid Era*, https://doi.org/10.1596/978-1-4648-1639-0. [6]

World Bank / CMI (2021), *Internationalization of Tertiary Education in MENA*, https://www.cmimarseille.org/knowledge-library/1-pager-internationalization-tertiary-education-mena-report. [26]

Notes

[1] In this chapter, MENA region or MENA countries refer to the group of countries that are members of the Union for the Mediterranean. These countries are: Algeria, Egypt, Jordan, Lebanon, Mauritania, Morocco, Palestinian Authority and Tunisia. Where the term "broad MENA region" is used, it refers to the group of MENA countries that include UfM and non-UfM members.

[2] It is considered that fixed broadband is more stable and faster than 4G (5G not being implemented yet in the MENA region, or marginally). In some emerging economies such as India fiber optics does not run through the territory and 99% of the internet goes via 4G and 5G.

[3] It is worth mentioning that the development of innovative teaching methods concerned also primary and secondary education. For example, Morocco proposed broadcasting classes on national TVs and distributed tablets to vulnerable children in rural areas.

3 Social affairs

The COVID-19 pandemic illustrated the dramatic consequences of having weak health and social protection systems as well as fragile supply chains of fundamental goods, notably food, when severe crises hit. This chapter highlights how existing weaknesses in MENA countries can increase the risk for crisis-induced poverty for many vulnerable groups, in particular informal workers, women and youth. It discusses policy solutions – including the promotion of a digital eco-system – to implement a growth model where decent jobs and career opportunities for all become the norm in MENA countries' labour markets.

Key takeaways

- In the MENA region the COVID-19 outbreak occurred in a context of weak health and social protection systems as well as weak supply chains of fundamental goods, notably food. Considering the large share of vulnerable groups in the population, in particular informal workers, women and youth, these existing weaknesses increase the risk that the pandemic induces poverty.
- MENA countries are historically characterised by low levels of social protection spending, varying on average between 2.5% and 7.6% of GDP compared to the OECD average of 20%. Following the coronavirus outbreak, governments in the region implemented successive rounds of relief and social assistance measures. Nevertheless, vulnerable communities were disproportionately affected.
- **The pandemic has exacerbated inequalities, creating a compounding effect on pre-existing vulnerabilities**. Baseline growth forecasts for the MENA region indicate that the share of population earning less than 5.5 USD per day could increase from about 174 million to 192 million by the end of 2021, potentially pushing 18 million people below the poverty threshold.
- **The pandemic put unprecedented stress on food supply chains, worsening food insecurity and malnutrition in the MENA region.** In 2020, those suffering from food insecurity in the total MENA population were approximately 12%, which is especially high given the overall for the world's total population is 6%.
- In the decades preceding the crisis, MENA countries made significant improvements in developing their health infrastructure, technology and human resources in both the public and private health sectors. Nevertheless, **MENA health systems were not prepared for a global pandemic.**
- **The pandemic revealed the importance of comprehensive data and information systems on social assistance.** Countries that had invested in their information systems were able to leverage them for rapid, high-coverage scale-up of social protection responses, while the lack of information limited the ability to reach marginalised groups. In this context, broad assistance responses, while quickly implemented, have shown their limitations, for instance by not being sufficiently gendered. As COVID-19 has accelerated the shift towards digital transformation, technology has an important role to play in enhancing vulnerable groups' access to social services.
- **Youth and women unemployment in the broad MENA region is among the highest in the world**. In the Southern Mediterranean, 70% of the working-age population is under 30 years old – a share expected to grow considerably. Due to the COVID-19 crisis, it is estimated that over half of the young people in the region moved to the informal sector. Moreover, the impact on young women's employment was more significant than on young men's. This occurred in a context where unemployment rates of young women are nearly double the rate of young men, due to legal and social barriers, as well as a lack of skills, e.g. digital skills, that limit women employability
- MENA governments should promote a digital eco-system to open new education and employment opportunities for youth and women as well as foster a culture of entrepreneurship and private sector development. Youth and women's empowerment should be a cornerstone of the recovery efforts to fully harness the contribution of young people and future generations in building sustainable growth – an economic growth model where decent jobs and career opportunities for all are a normality in the labour market.

Prior to the COVID-19 crisis, MENA countries[1] were characterised by relatively low levels of social protection spending, varying on average between 2.5% and 7.6% of GDP, compared to the OECD average of 20% (UN, 2020[1]). The pandemic exacerbated the risk of poverty and inequalities. Baseline growth forecasts for the region indicate that the share of the population earning less than USD 5.5 per day could increase from about 174 million to 192 million by the end of 2021. Thus, potentially 18 million people would be pushed below the poverty threshold because of COVID-19 (World Bank, 2021[2]).

To counter the increase in poverty, governments have been quick to take measures to maintain economies and provide social protection in response to rising unemployment induced by restrictions on mobility and economic activity. Countries, in the MENA region, implemented successive rounds of relief, and social protection measures, including social assistance, insurance, and labour market measures (OECD, 2020[3]). Nonetheless, many vulnerable groups with little official visibility could not be reached.

Vulnerabilities: health and social protection systems, food supply chains

Health systems were not prepared

In the decades preceding the pandemic, MENA countries made significant improvements in developing their health systems. Health infrastructure, technology and human resources have improved in the public and private health sectors, and countries including Egypt, Jordan, Lebanon and Tunisia have become regional medical hubs, serving foreign patients. The same countries developed free or low-cost health coverage (World Bank, 2021[4]). However, the COVID-19 crisis brought to light the limits of the region's health care systems, revealing their fragility and questioning their effectiveness. Indeed, despite recent progress, the region's level of preparedness to confront the global pandemic was not sufficient. Prior to the pandemic, health expenditures per capita reached 520 current USD on average in MENA countries, compared to an average of 4 885 current USD for OECD members. Moreover, in the region, health care remains to be largely provided through private facilities that charge fees. Low expenditures in public health relative to the public sector's wage bill seems to have shifted more of the financial burden of health care toward individuals (World Bank, 2021[4]). In general, across countries in the world, a persistent shortage of health workers and a high gap between investment in curative care at the expense of investment in preventive care is observed (OECD, 2021[5]).

Figure 3.1. Health expenditure per capita, selected regions and countries, 2000-18

Current USD

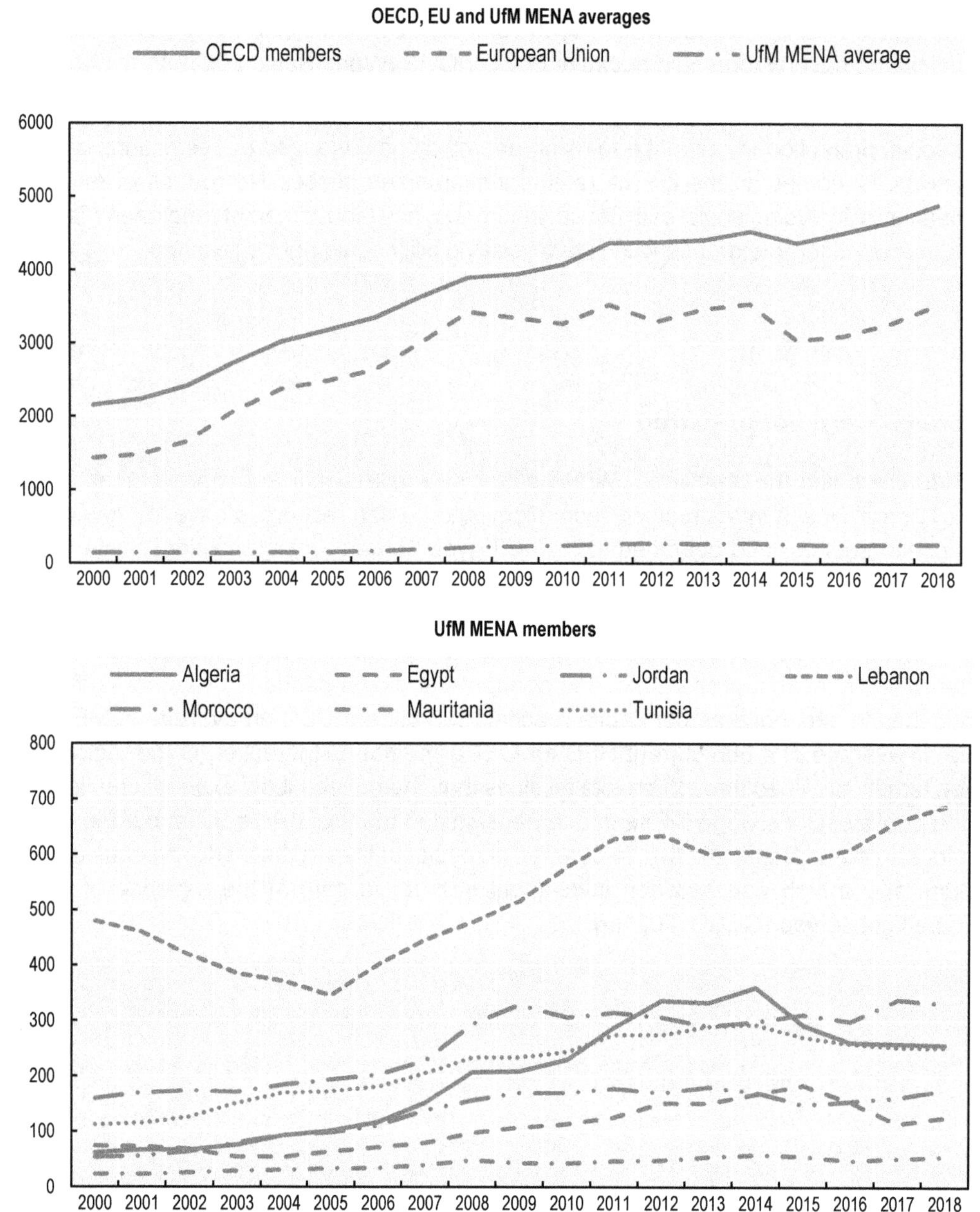

Note: Data for the Palestinian Authority are not available.

Source: World Development Indicators, https://data.worldbank.org/indicator/SH.XPD.CHEX.PC.CD?end=2018&locations=OE-DZ-EG-JO-LB-MR-MA-TN-PS-EU&start=2000 , World Health Organization Global Health Expenditure database 2021, https://apps.who.int/nha/database

Preparedness to deal with a pandemic varied across among MENA countries (OECD, 2020[6]), as also measured by the Global Health Security Index (Table 3.1). In 2019, while high-income countries featured an average score of 51.9, the average score for MENA countries was 36.2, slightly lower than the world average (40.2).

Table 3.1. Global Health Security Index, MENA countries, 2019

Score from 0 to 100

	Index score	Country ranking /195	Category
Algeria	23.4	173	Least prepared
Egypt	39.9	87	More prepared
Jordan	42.1	80	More prepared
Lebanon	43.1	73	More prepared
Mauritania	27.5	157	Least prepared
Morocco	43.7	68	More prepared
Tunisia	33.7	122	More prepared

Note: The GHS Index is a comprehensive assessment of global health security capabilities in 195 countries; data for the Palestinian Authority are not available. The country categories are: least prepared, more prepared, most prepared.
Source: GHS index 2019, https://www.ghsindex.org/about/

- Unlike many other countries in the broad MENA region, Jordan has taken a preventive approach to tackling the pandemic. The country was quick to introduce strict containment measures and enforcement before a certain number of COVID-19 confirmed cases and deaths were reached. Simultaneously, Jordan also undertook important investments in healthcare infrastructure and increased the number of medical personnel.
- However, health care systems in other MENA economies, such as Egypt and countries in the Maghreb region were particularly challenged and still face difficulties in preventing, detecting and responding to the virus. Systems were rapidly saturated and suffered from shortage of medical facilities and equipment, as well as a lack of human resources to deal with the pandemic.The number of medical personnel, nurses and midwives per 1 000 people is as low as 0.72 in Morocco and 0.79 in Egypt compared to 4.5 per 1000 people recommended by WHO (World Bank, 2020[7]). Moreover, the territorial concentration of hospitals and health care facilities in urban areas prevented the population living in rural and peripheral urban areas from accessing health care.
- In fragile areas such as in the Palestinian Authority, and to some extent Lebanon, the health care systems were unable to cope adequately with the COVID-19 outbreak. On the one hand, preventive measures are ineffective due to insufficient water, sanitation and hygiene services; on the other, the fragile economic situation of the population has to be balanced between the risk of infection and the inability to make a living (OECD, 2020[6]).

The pandemic also took a special toll on maternal health services, which includes antenatal care, delivery care and postnatal care services, with many countries in MENA reporting a drop in these services (UNICEF, 2021[8]).

Finally, during the pandemic, economic crisis risk factors generally associated with high level of stress – such as financial insecurity – have been exacerbated, while stabilising elements such as security of employment or access to health services have been limited by successive containment measures (OECD, 2021[9]). OECD studies show that in member countries, for which data exist, the mental situation of the unemployed and financially insecure was worse than that of the general population - a trend that predates the pandemic, but which appears to have accelerated with the COVID-19 outburst (OECD, 2021[10]). In the MENA region data are scarce, but a study involving a panel of more than 6000 citizens in 18 countries in the region found a similar trend, i.e. the pandemic brought a deterioration in the well-being of part of the adults in the region (Al Dhaheri et al., 2021[11]). The study suggests that the pandemic has eventually drawn attention to mental health awareness, which in turn translated into an increase in alertness among the health care professionals in identifying and targeting high-risk groups in the population, who are more at risk of developing mental health pathologies. Understanding of the strong causal links between people's psychological well-being, standard of living, and resilient health services made a significant improvement (OECD, 2021[10]).

COVID-19 exacerbated inequalities despite social protection measures

Social protection measures implemented to cope with the impacts of COVID-19 covered social assistance, social insurance and labour market programmes. Many of these measures were built on, and expanded, existing social protection policies, strategies and programmes (OECD, 2020[6]), (IMF, 2021[12]). Increasing coverage was implemented either through vertical expansion, where existing beneficiaries obtained additional benefits, or through horizontal expansion, which involves targeting additional beneficiaries especially in the more fragile populations often excluded from social coverage.

Due to the need to act quickly, many measures were not tailored, but had the advantage of being quick to implement and worked relatively well in the short term. Despite evidence of the socio-economic impact and burden of the pandemic on women, only 18% of the world's social protection responses were gender sensitive, i.e. addressing women's economic security and/or the increased burden of care (UN Women and UNDP, 2021[13]). This is a worldwide trend, recent data show women and girls are far less likely to receive COVID-19 relief than men (UN Women, 2022[14]). There is however a clear understanding of the need to implement targeted measures. In that regard, MENA countries were very active in dedicating gender sensitive relief in a fair share of the total measures adopted (Table 3.2.).

- An example of gender sensitive initiatives concerns Egypt, where the National Council for Women (NCW) reviewed all government measures for gender equality. It recently released the third version of a policy indicator to monitor measures and programmes undertaken in the context of the pandemic (OECD, 2020[3]).

Table 3.2. COVID-19 Policy responses in MENA region

Country	All measures	Gender sensitive	Unpaid care	Violence against women	Womens' economic security
Algeria	9	2	1		1
Egypt	48	25	4	12	9
Jordan	25	7	1	5	1
Lebanon	16	7		5	2
Mauritania	10	1			1
Morocco	22	9		5	4
Palestinian Authority	34	19	1	12	6
Tunisia	31	10		7	3

Source: (UN Women and UNDP, 2021[13]), https://data.undp.org/gendertracker/

Targeted responses have mainly focused on addressing the increase in violence against women. While this is a necessary action in the short term, it is important that gender considerations remain central also for economic reconstruction in the medium- to long-term. To date, few measures have specifically targeted women facing the economic repercussions of the crisis (UN Women, 2022[14]). In the MENA region, the majority of small business emergency relief policies do not fully reflect gender aspects of entrepreneurship. However, good practice examples of targeted measures on women's entrepreneurship exist and include cash transfers for women in Egypt and special paid leave in the Palestinian Authority. Governments have also offered support to women entrepreneurs, with the involvement of international organisations, often in the form of online training programmes (Egypt, Jordan). (IMF, 2021[12]).

The pandemic has also had serious consequences for ***refugees and internally displaced populations***, a majority of which are women (OECD, 2020[6]). The MENA region currently hosts the largest community of displaced populations in the world, particularly in Egypt, Lebanon and Jordan. Most refugee women have faced specific difficulties in accessing basic services, and have suffered violence and economic deprivation. Refugee girls have also been at greater risk of dropping out of school in addition to purely humanitarian considerations.

The responses to the crisis did not entirely address the social hardships experienced by ***the high numbers of informal workers***. Some countries, however, did introduce specific measures targeting informal workers; for instance:

- Egypt provided one-off monetary compensations (31.85 USD) to informal workers registered at the database for the Ministry of Manpower through post offices (Ministry of International Cooperation, 2020[15]).
- The Moroccan government addressed the informal sector by issuing a monthly mobile payment of 80-120 USD starting April 2020 to households that are beneficiaries of the Medical Assistance Scheme RAMED, a subsidized health insurance, and whose income has been affected by the health emergency rules. Households without RAMED operating in the informal sector and who have lost their income following compulsory confinement could also register online to receive cash support (OECD, 2020[16]).

The lack of comprehensive data on informal workers, however, complicates the development of adequate measures. It is possible that a large number of people severely impacted by COVID-19 could not benefit from the safeguards put in place, because of their non-existence in the administrative files of the competent social protection authorities.

The COVID-19 pandemic put unprecedented stress on food supply chains, worsening food insecurity and malnutrition in the MENA region (OECD, 2021[17]). Food insecurity in the MENA region is a growing challenge. Even before COVID-19, UN agencies estimated that over 51 million out of 465 million people within the broad MENA region were undernourished (UNICFEF, WFP, 2021[18]). Within the MENA countries covered by this report, approximately 13% of the population consumes insuficient ammount of food, as of May 2022. This situation is aggravated by the fact that countries in the region are among the world's largest food importers.

Overall, between October 2020 and January 2021, the number of people with insufficient food consumption increased in Algeria, Egypt, Lebanon, Morocco, Mauritania, the Palestinian Authority and Tunisia. Some countries stopped the exports of certain food products in 2020; e.g. Egypt suspended exports of all types of vegetables for 6 months in order to increase their strategic food reserves, and Algeria also banned several food products (IMF, 2021[12]). The trends for the early 2022 have shown a worsened prospect, as the proportion of people with insufficient food consumption has increased since the beginning of the year (Table 3.3), most likely due to the disruption in the food suply chains caused by the war in Ukraine. The levels remain higher than before the pandemic.

Table 3.3. Food insecurity in the MENA region amid COVID-19 crisis

	Population (million)	People with insufficient food consumption (million) (May 2022)	People with insufficient food consumption (million) (February 2022)	Food security trends (last 3 months : February -May 2022)	Import dependency % of cereals (2021)
Algeria	42.2	4.1	4.7	Decrease	69
Egypt	98.4	10.9	11.7	Decrease	55
Jordan	10	1.46	1.5	Decrease	100
Lebanon	6.8	1.27	1.3	Decrease	93
Mauritania	4.4	1.5	2.3	Decrease	71
Morocco	36	4.1	4.5	Decrease	50
Palestinian Authority	4.6	0.93	1	Decrease	100
Tunisia	11.6	1.32	1.3	Increase	66

Note: Food security trends represent the tendency observed over the last three months in the number of people with insufficient food consumption.
Source: World Food Programme 2022, https://hungermap.wfp.org/

Data show that the COVID-19 pandemic affected food-security in the MENA region to a greater extent that the rest of the world. Gender inequalities and discrimination against women and girls may potentially contribute to this fact. The gender disparity in access to food worldwide increased between 2018 and 2019 (FAO, IFAD, UNICEF, WFP and WHO, 2021[19]) and is expected to increase, as the pandemic and the measures taken to contain it impact negatively on food security and nutrition in different ways by gender (FAO, 2020[20]). While this is global, the MENA region is particularly (FAO, 2021[21]) due to the systemic limitations of the region's food supply chains.

Policy considerations

Supply chains should be reinforced to build resilience and address food insecurity in the region.

- *Mitigate the risk of the region's high dependence on food imports*, including risks related to fluctuating food prices. In addition, the region needs to address food losses at the top of the supply chain by improving the efficiency of food import and storage (World Bank, 2021[22]). MENA countries can capitalise on the example of Egypt. The country is implementing a modernisation of its food import control framework. The Egyptian National Food Safety Authority has implemented a risk-based regulatory policy. Food categories with a documented history of food safety compliance are less likely to be stopped for verification and sampling upon arrival in Egypt therefore the risk of delays is mitigated and overall the system facilitates the flow of food products.
- *Increase the capacity of local agricultural productions as an engine of growth*, including for vulnerable populations (women and migrants), who are highly represented in this sector of activity. The region should invest in advanced practices and technologies adapted to a changing climate, such as hydroponics, conservation agriculture and the safe use of treated water. Digital technology in the agri-food sector should be at the heart of all strategies of post-COVID-19 reconstruction. This is especially important for developing new financial models to leverage private investment in agriculture if public spending and other policies are reviewed by governments. Development interventions are needed to help farmers adopt more productive and sustainable systems that are resilient to drought, floods and other risks.
- *Advance gender equality and the empowerment of women and girls to enhance food security,* essential to achieving the goals of the 2030 Agenda for Sustainable Development including the ones related to food security. To guide progress in this area the CFS decided to develop Voluntary Guidelines on Gender Equality and the Empowerment of Women and Girls in the Context of Food Security and Nutrition (FAO, 2021[23]). CFS Guidelines aim to assist governments, development partners and other stakeholders to advance gender equality in their efforts to eradicate hunger and malnutrition. Governments in the UfM should consider following the said recommendations to improve structurally their alimentary resilience via a sound policy framework.

Data are key. The pandemic has demonstrated the need for reliable data systems to support transparent and effective decision-making.

- *Improve data on health systems*. In MENA countries, there is urgent need to overhaul data systems as part of health systems reform, and to foster a culture of data openness and use. One example of relevant use of data is the case of screening capacity, a crucial element of health surveillance that is essential for disease prevention and response (de Walque, 2020[24]). The COVID-19 crisis highlighted the importance of good mental well-being as a driver of recovery, but the pandemic also highlighted gaps in targeting support (OECD, 2021[10]). In MENA countries, it is difficult to identify the extent of action required as there is little large-scale data. Thus, while decisive action to reduce the impact of COVID on mental illness is well envisaged as essential for sustainable economic recovery, it is rarely measured. An effort must therefore be made to develop indicators.
- *Improve data on social protection*. Countries that had invested in their information systems were able to leverage them for rapid, high-coverage scale-up of social protection responses (SPACE,

2021[25]). The incomplete coverage of existing information systems has limited the ability to reach some marginalised groups. Strengthening information systems is therefore critical to build better systems for the future and will require investment over the next few years. The window of opportunity to ensure the development of inclusive information systems is now (GIZ, 2019[26]).

- UfM members that have already launched programmes to implement these types of tools, such as Egypt, Jordan, Mauritania, Tunisia and Palestinian Authority (ESCWA, 2019[27]), should capitalise on the achievements and develop them into more integrated systems.
- The Moroccan Single Social Register (RSU) is to be launched in 2022, and will function as a one-stop application portal for all the country's administrations. Households will register with the RSU and update their data. The agency that manages the RSU will provide data on eligible beneficiaries to implementers of social programmes. The programme is planned to operate in conjunction with the National Population Register (NPR). The basic identification numbers provided by the NPR will be the basis for the registration of potential beneficiaries in the RSU (Ministry of Culture, 2021[28]).
- As COVID-19 has accelerated the shift towards digital transformation, there is a possibility that in the long-term, access to social services and assistance will shift to remote documentation and registration.

- *Improve knowledge of impact of relief measures*. The shortcomings in data systems in the MENA region is compounded by insufficient knowledge about the efficiency of social relief measures on economies and target populations. In many countries across both the developed and developing world, this led governments to embark on numerous regulatory measures to protect the population from the pandemic based on "trial and error". For instance, despite the strength of evidence on social protection as an effective poverty reduction instrument, there is still little indication on which types of instruments deliver which types of outcomes for different groups (ODI, 2020[29]). There is even more limited evidence on how women and men respond differently to shocks, what gendered information should be collected for early warning purposes, or how social protection information systems can generate information for inclusive decision-making (SPACE, 2021[25]). Only now, considering the amount of measures introduced around the world, a comprehensive ex-post analysis is possible.
- *Produce gender- and age-disaggregated crisis data* that address both the need for social support, targeted economic recovery and health (Gatti et al., 2021[30]) to depart from one-size-fits-all social policies that will not be sustainable in the long-term. Therefore, all institutions collecting crisis data should not only expand their work but also integrate a gender perspective, along with other cross-cutting elements of vulnerability e.g. rural-urban disparities. The OECD has identified two different levels of action as priorities, i.e. extend the spectrum of data collection on the subject and integrate gender sensitive data.
- *Promote the implementation of digital technologies*. Better understanding of needs and a rationalised relief can be achieved due to new digital technologies. The latter play an important role in crisis response. Vulnerable groups' access to and use of technology should be of particular importance. Digital technologies help state authorities reach remote groups traditionally excluded from social assistance schemes, i.e. through the introduction of e-wallets and mobile applications for money transfer.
- *Consider the long-term effects of the pandemic on vulnerable groups of the MENA's population*. MENA economies should, in particular, reflect on how to take advantage of the impetus created by the necessity to survive the crisis, to build long-term perspectives on how making progress against the Sustainable Development Goals (especially goals 1-5 and 10). The COVID-19 crisis has amplified the vulnerability of some groups, but the initiatives taken for the recovery could pave the way for a better future.

- *Sustain regional and national efforts to develop resilient health care systems* by continuing their investment measures, creating innovation opportunities and boosting the research and development sector. In this way, strengthening the role of the private sector and enhancing public-private partnerships is key. In Morocco for example, public-private partnership between the Ministry of Industry and various private sector companies enabled the development of locally produced Intensive Care Unit beds, easier to acquire than those imported from abroad (OECD, 2020[6]). The private sector is particularly important in providing services in areas facing political and civil unrest, where government services are unavailable or saturated.

Opportunities: digital economy and women and youth economic empowerment

The economic slowdown resulting from the COVID-19 crisis exacerbated the vulnerability of women and youth in the MENA region, for whom unemployment was already particularly high before the pandemic (Table 3.4).

Table 3.4. MENA unemployment rate, by age and gender

		Total	Men	Women	
Algeria	Unemployment rate (%)	13.6	10.8	26.2	2017
	Youth (%)	39.3	33.1	82.0	2017
Egypt	Unemployment rate (%)	7.8	4.8	21.6	2019
	Youth (%)	19.2	12.2	49.3	2019
Jordan	Unemployment rate (%)	16.8	15.4	24.1	2019
	Youth (%)	37.3	34.8	49.4	2019
Lebanon	Unemployment rate (%)	11.3	10	14.3	2019
	Youth (%)	23.4	24.5	21.4	2019
Mauritania	Unemployment rate (%)	10.3	9.7	11.4	2017
	Youth (%)	21.1	18.8	24.9	2017
Morocco	Unemployment rate (%)	9.3	8.8	10.7	2016
	Youth (%)	22.2	22	22.8	2016
Palestinian Authority	Unemployment rate (%)	25.9	22.5	40.1	2020
	Youth (%)	42.1	36.6	70.0	2020
Tunisia	Unemployment rate (%)	15.1	12.3	22.2	2019
	Youth (%)	34.9	33.8	37.2	2017

Note: Latest data available, ILO estimates
Source: ILOSTAT 2021, https://ilostat.ilo.org/data/country-profiles/

The youth population is expected to grow by 40% to almost 600 million by 2030 (Middle East Institute, 2019[31]). Up to 80% of youth in the region work in the informal sector, and they are more likely to be under temporary contracts, often in sectors that have been severely hit by the crisis such as travel and tourism and restauration sectors (OECD, 2021[32]).

It is estimated that women in the larger Arab world will lose approximately 700,000 jobs as a result of the pandemic (ESCWA, 2020[33]). The effects of the pandemic on women and men workers are also dependent on the sector and conditions of their employment, which typically differ for male and female workers (Figure 3.2). In the private sector within the broad MENA region, women represent a significant share of the workforce in the low segments of the manufacturing industry, which was severely affected by disruptions from both supply and demand shocks.

- In Tunisia, 26% of women are employed in the manufacturing sector, where they are over-represented in low-skilled and low-paying sectors such as the textile sector (OECD, 2020[3]) which came to a full stop during many months in the course of the pandemic.
- Women are highly susceptible to hold insecure, part-times jobs: data estimates that 47% and 48% of women hold part-time jobs in labour markets such as Morocco and the Palestinian Authority, respectively (ILO, 2020[34]).
- Nearly 62% of all female workers are informally employed in the MENA region (ILO data) (OECD, 2020[3]).

Figure 3.2. Employment in MENA countries, 2018

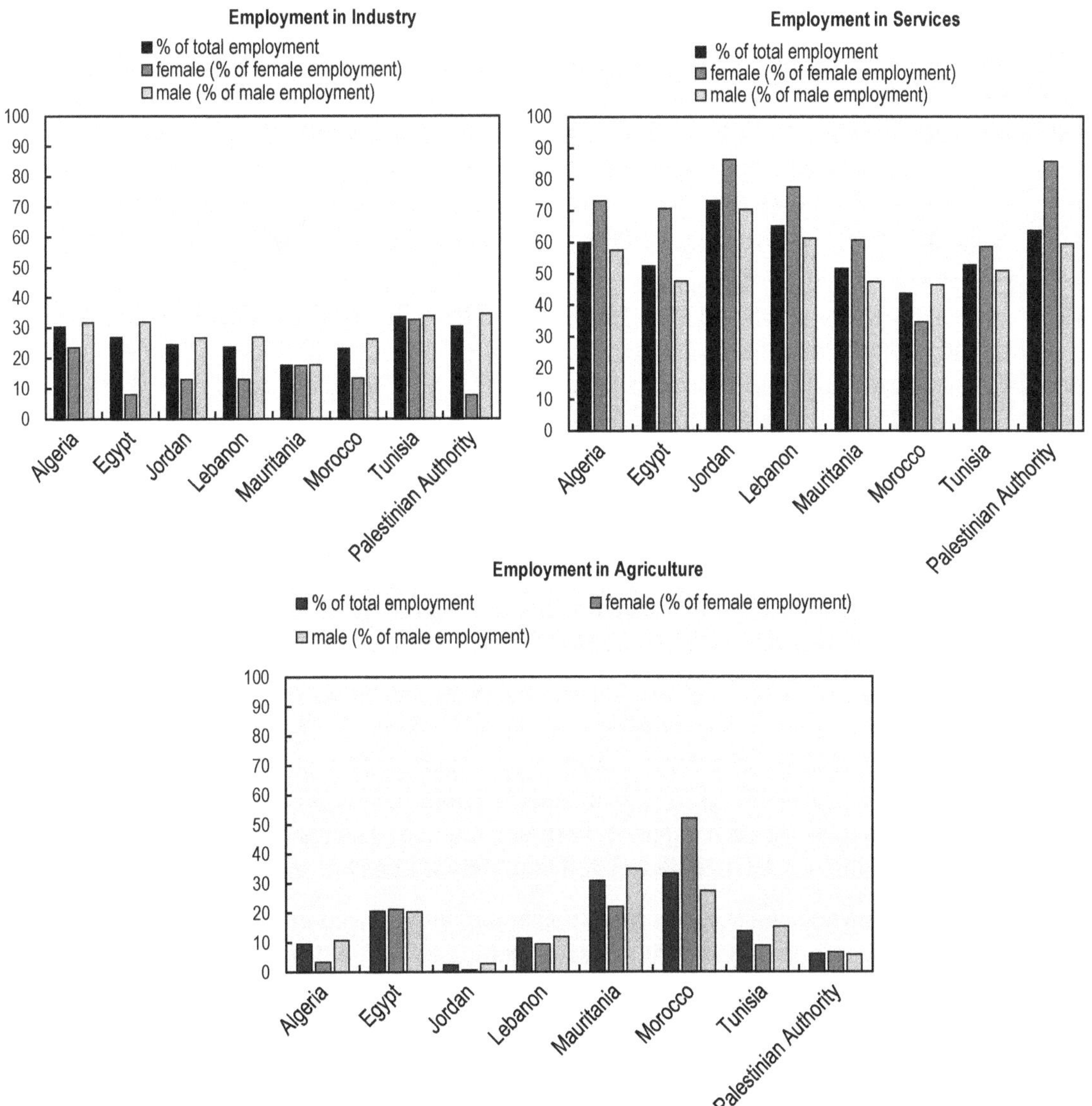

Note: This is a modelled ILO estimate. The series is part of the ILO estimates and is harmonized to ensure comparability across countries and over time by accounting for differences in data source, scope of coverage, methodology, and other country-specific factors. The estimates are based mainly on nationally representative labour force surveys, with other sources (population censuses and nationally reported estimates) used only when no survey data are available. Estimates for countries with very limited labour market information have a high degree of uncertainty. Hence, estimates for countries with limited nationally reported data should not be considered as "observed" data, and great care needs to be applied when using these data for analysis, especially at the country level.
Source: International Labour Organization, ILOSTAT database. https://ilostat.ilo.org/data/

The fourth industrial revolution opens new employment and learning opportunities to youth and women. COVID-19 accelerated the ongoing digitalisation of production processes and adoption of digital technology across businesses, as well as the intensity and extent to which businesses use digital technologies to maintain operations. Teleworking and distance learning have become standard good practice, instead of being episodic or second-best solutions.

Indeed, digital technologies can significantly facilitate access to higher education and, ultimately, enhance skills acquisition and employability of youth and women (see chapter 2). In parallel, digital technologies create new job opportunities, including via entrepreneurial ventures that build on digital tools. For instance, further development of tools for online payment and e-commerce can facilitate trade across borders and possibly enable young and women entrepreneurs in the region to reach distant markets despite the numerous constraints (e.g. limited financial resources, social attitudes, location in rural or isolated areas) these entrepreneurs might experience.

Furthermore, by virtue of digital technologies, businesses can be created that are less capital and labour-intensive than traditional ones, requiring less space for offices and production. In MENA countries, being able to dispense with the need for expensive real estate could make a difference to young and women entrepreneurs for whom access to finance can be difficult and where women face problems in leasing and owning property. Finally, the possibility of digital technologies to manage entrepreneurial projects from home offers a compromise between paid work and family responsibilities which play a pivotal role in women's labour participation in the region.

In the MENA region, the share of women in professional and technical jobs is expected to double by 2030 through digitisation, online platforms and entrepreneurship (McKinsey & Company, 2020[35]). However, enhancing women's digital skills and access to technology is a necessary but not sufficient step. Despite representing 34% to 57% of science, technology, engineering and mathematics (STEM) graduates and outperforming boys in digital skills, few MENA women pursue their careers in STEM occupations or entrepreneurship (OECD WEEF, 2021[36]). Even the best female performers in mathematics and science do not favour careers in STEM fields.

- In Lebanon for example, among students with high scores in mathematics or science, over 46% of boys reported the desire to be employed in science and engineering professions in the future, compared to only 26% of girls (OECD, 2021[37]).

A UNIDO study conducted on 1,400 women entrepreneurs in the broad MENA region manufacturing sector, revealed that few of them are leveraging the new opportunities offered by digital technologies. Around a quarter of respondents report the use of digital technologies at some stage in the design, manufacturing and selling processes of their businesses. Information and Communication Technology (ICT) usage is mostly limited to the commercial sphere and the use of social networks as an extension of private use. Furthermore, the survey revealed limited familiarity with any concepts related to Industry 4.0.

Structural gender issues (including limited access to finance, network and information; lack of mentoring and role models, social norms and gender stereotypes) combined with a digital gender gap, threatens to exclude women from the fourth industrial revolution. In recent years, women were still 20% less likely than men to have a senior leadership position in the mobile communication industry. Evidence from the Union of Arab ICT Associations suggests that while women in the MENA region represent up to 30% of the ICT workforce, they only hold 9% of the ICT high management positions (OECD WEEF, 2021[36]). More equal gender representation is important to ensure gender-sensitivity in the design of products and services and in addressing user needs.

Policy considerations

As discussed above, analysing how general fiscal and monetary measures may affect young entrepreneurs and women-owned businesses will help identify unintended gaps, in order to design more sensitive medium- and long-term economic recovery strategies (OECD, 2020[38]). The design and implementation of COVID-19 recovery plans should capitalise on positive experiences reflected in the emergence of new women-led micro-businesses. This has been seen for instance in Lebanon, where new businesses appeared in the *social and solidarity economy* (e.g. cooking and distribution services), mostly set up by women who had lost their jobs because of the financial crisis in Lebanon prior to the COVID-19 pandemic (OECD, 2020[3]).

The points below highlight a series of features for youth and gender-sensitive policy initiatives:

- *Promote a digital eco-system to open new education and employment opportunities for youth and women.* This is in line with the UfM Mediterranean Initiative for Jobs (Med4Jobs) (UfM, 2019[39]), which aims to increase employability of young people and women, close the gap between labour demand and supply, and foster a culture of entrepreneurship and private sector development. Youth and women empowerment should be a cornerstone of the recovery efforts to fully harness the contribution of young people and future generations in building sustainable growth – an economic growth model where decent jobs and career opportunities are the norm in the labour market.
- *Improving access to finance.* This may include dedicated funding streams or dedicated shares of lending programmes. Access to public procurement is also possible based on well-defined criteria, such as price preferences on threshold procurement.
- *Increase business advice and counselling for youth and women entrepreneurs.* This can include advice on how to stabilise ailing businesses and help new entrepreneurs' grow their businesses. Promote the resilience of existing businesses in addition to creation seems particularly appropriate in a context of crisis. Equally important is to facilitate the development of a pool of women entrepreneurs as advisors and mentors, and encourage an increase in the representation of women among business angels and managers of venture capital funds.
- *Help maintain networks of entrepreneurs open to youth and women.* Networking can be effective for the entrepreneurial ecosystem, improving access to markets, finance, knowledge and suppliers. In the context of COVID-19, face-to-face events have been cancelled and networking organisations may need financial and technical support to survive and also create online activities.

References

de Walque, D. (2020), *How Two Tests Can Help Contain COVID-19 and Revive the Economy*, https://openknowledge.worldbank.org/handle/10986/33583. [24]

ESCWA (2020), *The impact of COVID-19 on Gender Equality in the Arab Region*, https://www2.unwomen.org/-/media/field%20office%20arab%20states/attachments/publications/2020/04/impact%20of%20covid%20on%20gender%20equality%20-%20policy%20brief.pdf?la=en&vs=4414. [33]

ESCWA (2019), *Social Protection Reforms in Arab Countries*, https://www.un.org/unispal/wp-content/uploads/2019/10/E.ESCWA_.ADD_.2019.1.pdf. [27]

FAO (2021), "CFS 2021/49/10 - CFS Voluntary Guidelines on Gender Equality and Women's and Girls' Empowerment in the Context of Food Security and Nutrition – Draft Conclusions", https://www.fao.org/publications/card/en/c/NG687EN/. [23]

FAO (2021), *Enhancing resilience of food systems in the Arab States ; Near East and North Africa Regional Overview of Food Security and Nutrition 2020*, https://www.unicef.org/mena/media/12021/file/Near%20East%20and%20North%20Africa%20Regional%20Overview%20of%20Food%20Security%20and%20Nutrition%202020.pdf.pdf. [21]

FAO (2020), *Gendered impacts of COVID-19 and equitable policy responses in agriculture, food security and nutrition*, http://www.fao.org/documents/card/en/c/ca9198en. [20]

FAO, IFAD, UNICEF, WFP and WHO (2021), *The State of Food Security and Nutrition in the World 2021*, FAO, IFAD, UNICEF, WFP and WHO, https://doi.org/10.4060/cb4474en. [19]

Gatti, R. et al. (2021), *MENA ECONOMIC UPDATE APRIL 2021: How Institutions Shape the Tradeoff between Short-Term Needs and Long-Term Costs of Public Debt in Middle East and North Africa*, The World Bank, https://doi.org/10.1596/978-1-4648-1699-4. [30]

GIZ (2019), *Building an integrated and digital social protection information system*, https://www.giz.de/en/downloads/giz2019-en-integrated-digital-social-protection-information-system.pdf. [26]

ILO (2020), *Incidence of part-time employment by sex*, https://www.ilo.org/shinyapps/bulkexplorer54/?lang=en&segment=indicator&id=EMP_PTER_SEX_RT_A. [34]

IMF (2021), *Policy Response to COVID-19 - Policy Tracker*, https://www.imf.org/en/Topics/imf-and-covid19/Policy-Responses-to-COVID-19. [12]

Mahapatra, B. (ed.) (2021), "Impact of COVID-19 on mental health and quality of life: Is there any effect? A cross-sectional study of the MENA region", *PLOS ONE*, Vol. 16/3, p. e0249107, https://doi.org/10.1371/journal.pone.0249107. [11]

McKinsey & Company (2020), *Women at work: Job opportunities in the Middle East set to double with the Fourth Industrial Revolution*, https://www.mckinsey.com/~/media/mckinsey/featured%20insights/middle%20east%20and%20africa/women%20at%20work%20in%20the%20middle%20east/women-at-work-in-the-middle-east.pdf. [35]

Middle East Institute (2019), *Freshwater Resources in the MENA Region: Risks and Opportunit*, https://www.mei.edu/publications/freshwater-resources-mena-region-risks-and-opportunities#:~:text=In%202018%2c%20the%20region%20had%2c1.7%20percent%20as%20of%202017.&text=The%20region%27s%20population%20is%20projected%2cand%20731%20million%20by%202050. [31]

Ministry of Culture (2021), *House of Advisors Approves Framework Bill on Social Protection*, https://www.maroc.ma/en/news/house-advisors-approves-framework-bill-social-protection. [28]

Ministry of International Cooperation (2020), *COVID-19 Response & Rebuild*, https://drive.google.com/file/d/1a2IaAE6Jw38WwgaNSfoguthv29gYUaon/view. [15]

ODI (2020), *Social protection and the future work : A gender analysis*, https://cdn.odi.org/media/documents/Social_protection_and_the_future_of_work_a_gender_analysis.pdf. [29]

OECD (2021), *A New Benchmark for Mental Health Systems: Tackling the Social and Economic Costs of Mental Ill-Health*, OECD Health Policy Studies, OECD Publishing, Paris, https://doi.org/10.1787/4ed890f6-en. [10]

OECD (2021), "COVID-19 and food systems: Short- and long-term impacts", *OECD Food, Agriculture and Fisheries Papers*, No. 166, OECD Publishing, Paris, https://doi.org/10.1787/69ed37bd-en. [17]

OECD (2021), *Health at a Glance 2021: OECD Indicators*, OECD Publishing, Paris, https://doi.org/10.1787/ae3016b9-en. [5]

OECD (2021), *OECD Policy Responses to Coronavirus (COVID-19) : Tackling the mental health impact of the COVID-19 crisis: An integrated, whole-of-society response*, https://www.oecd.org/coronavirus/policy-responses/tackling-the-mental-health-impact-of-the-covid-19-crisis-an-integrated-whole-of-society-response-0ccafa0b/. [9]

OECD (2021), *Social resilience: moving away from informality to formal*, https://www.oecd.org/mena/competitiveness/issue-paper-session-4.pdf. [32]

OECD (2021), *Women's Economic Empowerment Forum (WEEF) - Gender-sensitive education and skills development policies in the MENA*, https://www.oecd.org/mena/competitiveness/WEEF-Webinar-Conclusions-5-July-2021-Digital-skills.pdf. [37]

OECD (2020), *OECD Policy Responses to Coronavirus (COVID-19) : COVID-19 crisis in MENA countries*, https://www.oecd.org/coronavirus/policy-responses/covid-19-crisis-response-in-mena-countries-4b366396/. [6]

OECD (2020), *OECD Policy Responses to Coronavirus (COVID-19) : COVID-19 crisis in the MENA region: impact on gender equality and policy responses*, https://www.oecd.org/coronavirus/policy-responses/covid-19-crisis-in-the-mena-region-impact-on-gender-equality-and-policy-responses-ee4cd4f4/. [3]

OECD (2020), *The COVID-19 crisis in Morocco*, https://www.oecd.org/mena/competitiveness/The-Covid-19-Crisis-in-Morocco.pdf. [16]

OECD (2020), *Women enterprise policy and COVID-19: Towards a gender - sensitive response*, https://www.oecd.org/cfe/leed/OECD_Webinar_Women_Entrepreneurship_Policy_and_COVID-19_Summary.pdf. [38]

OECD WEEF (2021), *Gender-sensitive education and skills development policies in the MENA region*, https://www.oecd.org/mena/competitiveness/Agenda.pdf. [36]

SPACE (2021), *Inclusive Information Systems for Social Protection: Intentionally Integrating Gender and Disability*, https://socialprotection.org/sites/default/files/publications_files/SPACE_Inclusive%20Information%20Systems%20for%20Social%20Protection_Intentionally%20Integrating%20Gender%20and%20Disability.pdf. [25]

UfM (2019), *Med4Jobs: Creating Job Opportunities Promoting Inclusive Growth*, https://ufmsecretariat.org/wp-content/uploads/2017/12/LeafletMed4Jobs_2019_WEB.pdf. [39]

UN (2020), *Social protection responses to the COVID-19 crisis in the MENA/Arab States region*, https://socialprotection.org/sites/default/files/publications_files/MENA%20COVID19%20brief%20-%20FINAL_v4.pdf. [1]

UN Women (2022), *Women and Girls Left Behind : Glaring Gaps in Pandemic Responses*, https://data.unwomen.org/sites/default/files/documents/Publications/glaring-gaps-response-RGA.pdf. [14]

UN Women and UNDP (2021), *COVID-19 Global Gender Response Tracker*, https://data.undp.org/gendertracker/. [13]

UNICEF (2021), *Middle East and North Africa Region COVID-19 Situation Report No.13*, https://www.unicef.org/mena/media/10841/file/UNICEF%20MENARO%20COVID-19%20Situation%20Report%20No.13%20-%20End%20of%20Year%202020_0.pdf%20.pdf. [8]

UNICFEF, WFP (2021), *Near East and North Africa Regional Overview of Food Security and Nutrition*, https://www.unicef.org/mena/reports/enhancing-resilience-food-systems-arab-states. [18]

World Bank (2021), *MENA Crisis Tracker - 27 September 2021*, https://documents1.worldbank.org/curated/en/280131589922657376/pdf/MENA-Crisis-Tracker-September-27-2021.pdf. [2]

World Bank (2021), "MENA Has a Food Security Problem, But There Are Ways to Address It", https://www.worldbank.org/en/news/opinion/2021/09/24/mena-has-a-food-security-problem-but-there-are-ways-to-address-it. [22]

World Bank (2021), *Overconfident: How Economic and Health Fault Lines Left the Middle East and North Africa Ill-Prepared to Face COVID-19*, https://openknowledge.worldbank.org/bitstream/handle/10986/36318/9781464817984.pdf. [4]

World Bank (2020), *Mitigating the Impact of COVID-19 and Strengthening Health Systems in the Middle East and North Africa*, https://openknowledge.worldbank.org/handle/10986/34238?show=full&locale-attribute=es. [7]

Notes

[1] In this chapter, MENA region or MENA countries refer to the group of countries that are members of the Union for the Mediterranean. These countries are: Algeria, Egypt, Jordan, Lebanon, Mauritania, Morocco, Palestinian Authority and Tunisia. Where the term "broad MENA region" is used, it refers to the group of MENA countries that include UfM and non-UfM members.

4 Water, environment and the blue economy

The COVID-19 pandemic exacerbated water-stress and food insecurity in the MENA region, the world's most water scarce region. This chapter analyses trends in infrastructure investments in the water and waste sectors in MENA countries, as well as employment opportunities in these sectors, driven by urbanisation, tourism development, irrigated agriculture and industrialisation. It highlights that the economic recovery offers an opportunity to integrate environmental fiscal reforms into policy reform agendas to maximise integration of social and environmental benefits.

Key takeaways

- During the pandemic, countries in the MENA region have not been able to take full advantage of containment and health preservation measures, as nearly 66 million people in the broad MENA region lack basic sanitation services, facilitating greater opportunities for the spread of disease. Similarly, about 82% of the region's wastewater is not treated nor reused, while less than half of wastewater is simply treated, cutting the region off from a sustainable and cost-effective source of water that can be recycled for purposes such as agricultural and landscape irrigation, industrial processes, and non-potable urban applications. Eventually, the difficulty in obtaining significant results from COVID-19 mitigation measures has revealed a lack of access to water that is safe to drink.
- The pandemic has exacerbated water-stress and food insecurity for the world's most water scarce region. To counteract the shortages of imported food that characterised the downturn in agricultural trade in the early months of the pandemic, MENA countries had to re-allocate extra water resources to agricultural production in order to boost their local food output. The resulting water stress, however, has further undermined the region's fragile overall water resource management.
- Estimates of water use during COVID-19 ranged from 9 to 12 additional litres of water per person per day due to changes in behaviour and consumption patterns, as well as increased expenditures and domestic water demand relative to industrial and agricultural water uses, representing an additional investment of USD 150-250 million per month to meet the additional water needs.
- The MENA region's growth, driven by urbanisation, tourism development, irrigated agriculture and industrialisation prior to the pandemic has opened up employment opportunities in the water sector. The strategic water sector in the broad MENA region, while still timidly aligned with new technologies, offers great potential for employment of specialists in ICT who will fully push the sector into the digital era.
- Investment in infrastructure projects in the MENA plummeted. Although infrastructural investments decreased in comparison to previous years, new investments in the water and waste sectors are still being signed, albeit at a slower pace and mostly through development banks.
- Initiatives to curb marine plastic pollution started to take form in the region, but further efforts are needed in order to improve the waste management systems and make them more effective as well as develop. Strategic initiatives to curb marine plastic pollution are being hampered by increased need for single-use plastic products coupled with ineffective waste collection systems. The MENA region is particularly stuck in the systematic failures of plastic value chain that do not hold producers accountable.
- COVID-19 protocols provided temporary relief for the Mediterranean's water and land environments and biodiversity, but incorporating green policies in recovery packages will be crucial for sustainability. The decrease in activity on the coasts from business closures and a decrease in visitors on beaches have protected, to a certain extent, the marine environment from forms of pollution such as plastics, hydrocarbon spillage, microbiological loads, and noise levels. However, COVID-19 related plastic waste such as masks and gloves have increased and become a new challenge.
- Economic recovery offers the opportunity to integrate Environmental Fiscal Reforms into policy reform agendas to maximise integration of social and environmental benefits.

Water action

COVID-19 has exacerbated water-stress and food insecurity for the world's most water scarce region

The broad MENA region[1] is considered the most water scarce region in the world, with a large portion of the region's population living underwater scarcity or absolute scarcity. Of the 18 countries in the broad MENA region, five are classified as water scarce and 11 others are considered as absolutely scarce, indicating that up to 86% of the region's population lives underwater shortages. While 70% of global water is used for agricultural purposes, the number reaches more than 80% in the MENA region, meaning water-scarcity has a particularly severe effect on the region's agricultural output and food-security.

Figure 4.1. Drinking water management in MENA countries, 2015-20

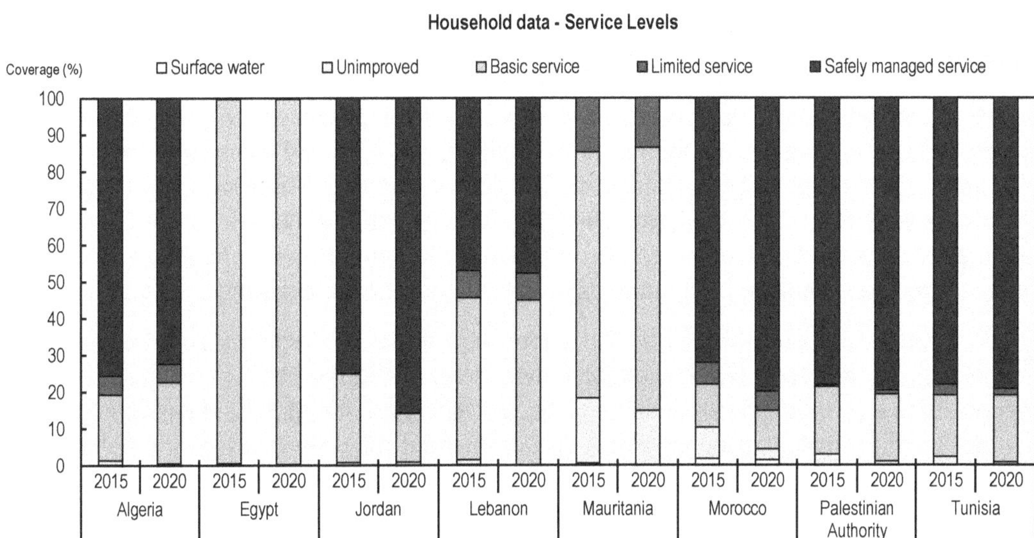

Source: World Health Organisation, https://washdata.org/data/household#!/dashboard/new.

The MENA region suffers from poor water management, deteriorating or out-dated water infrastructure and issues with governance, leading to large strains on the agricultural sector. Some of these problems are related to fiscal constraints and regulatory issues. For example, OECD (2014) *Water Governance in Jordan* highlighted fragmented and unclear responsibilities for oversight, a lack of efficient approach to tariff regulation and patchy performance monitoring, and recommended a high-quality regulatory framework to achieve good levels of service provision at an affordable cost for society.

In the context of the pandemic, water stress has increased due to a greater allocation of water resources to the agriculture sector in an effort to offset lower food exports in countries where agricultural products, especially wheat of which the Arab region imports 65% of its total stocks, are a large share of exports and to counterbalance shortages of imported food (UN ESCWA, 2020[1]). Indeed, with 55 million of its 456.7 million population undernourished, about 12% of the population, the broad MENA region also has one of the highest rates of food insecurity in the world. The pandemic has aggravated these circumstances, increasing the number of acutely food insecure people in MENA from 6% of the region's population to approximately 20%. Marginalised populations such as refugees are especially vulnerable to food insecurity and the pandemic has severely impacted this group; for instance, in 2020 a quarter of the Syrian refugees in Jordan and half of Syrian refugee households in Lebanon were in immediate need of food and water (Belhaj and Soliman, 2021[2]).

In addition to infrastructural deficiencies and aggravated social challenges, the region is also having to contend with environmental challenges, like climate change, that make feeding a growing population particularly difficult. An increase in the frequency of extreme weather and higher temperatures is affecting local agriculture. Half of the population of the broad MENA region already lives under conditions of water stress; with the population expected to grow to nearly 700 million in 2050, per capita water availability will be halved. The year 2020 also saw one of the worst desert locust outbreaks in over 23 countries, including Yemen and Djibouti, affecting livelihoods and food security for millions of people. (Soliman, 2021[3])

Prior to the pandemic, in connection with climate change, the main challenges in combatting food insecurity in the region were a rapidly growing population with 66% of people expected to be living in urban areas by 2030 (see Chapter 5), and high dependence on imports for well-balanced diets. Sudden disruption in agro-food global value chains caused by the closure of restaurants, markets and hotels has also had a devastating effect on the fishing industry for countries bordering the Mediterranean. Limited supplies of protective material for producers and processing workers, scarcity in supplies, and logistical challenges are further complicating the harvest and export of fresh produce worldwide, especially in the fishing sector (FAO, 2020[4]).

The broad MENA region is also a prime example of the logistical difficulties faced by both sides of the food production chain due to the pandemic. For example, while fishing exports in the region have significantly declined, the drop in fishery for North Sea Brown Shrimp in Germany has also affected the processing phase that takes place in Morocco (OECD, 2020[5]). Meanwhile, employment subsidies and policy measures to ease the strain on personnel affected by the pandemic are unsuitable for small-scale fishers that are often self-employed without registered income or health insurance (UNCTAD, 2020[6])

The scope to improve the quality of agricultural jobs and make the region's agri-food sector more attractive is wide. The need for a skilled workforce evidenced during the pandemic should be a sign for MENA economies to step up digital skills and vocational training for infrastructural positions, particularly in water sector maintenance and management. The sentiment for better-trained and better-equipped personnel for the water sector has also been echoed in MENA economies, for example Morocco, where training in entrepreneurship and climate-smart practices are taking place (Belhaj and Soliman, 2021[2]).

*Lack of **sanitation and wastewater infrastructure** has impeded the region's pandemic mitigation measures*

- COVID-19 has revealed the importance of access to clean water supplies and services during pandemics, and how volatility or a lack thereof can have critical implications for both the effectiveness of crisis response efforts and for promoting growth and building resilience in a post-pandemic world. In many communities around the world, a lack of reliable and affordable water supply and sanitation services deprives people of their most basic protections against the spread of the virus. Prior to the pandemic, the WHO had reported that improving water, sanitation, and hygiene (WASH) conditions has the potential to prevent at least 9.1% of the global disease burden and 6.3% of all deaths (Prüss-Üstün et al., 2008[7]).

After the pandemic began to take off, areas in the broad MENA region that already lacked safe sanitation services now also faced limited handwashing opportunities as a mechanism to mitigate the spread of infectious diseases, such as COVID-19 (Sadoff and Smith, 2020[8]). Nearly 66 million people in the broad MENA region lack basic sanitation and hygiene services, facilitating greater chances of disease spreading (Figure 4.2).

Figure 4.2. Sanitation management levels in MENA countries, 2015-20

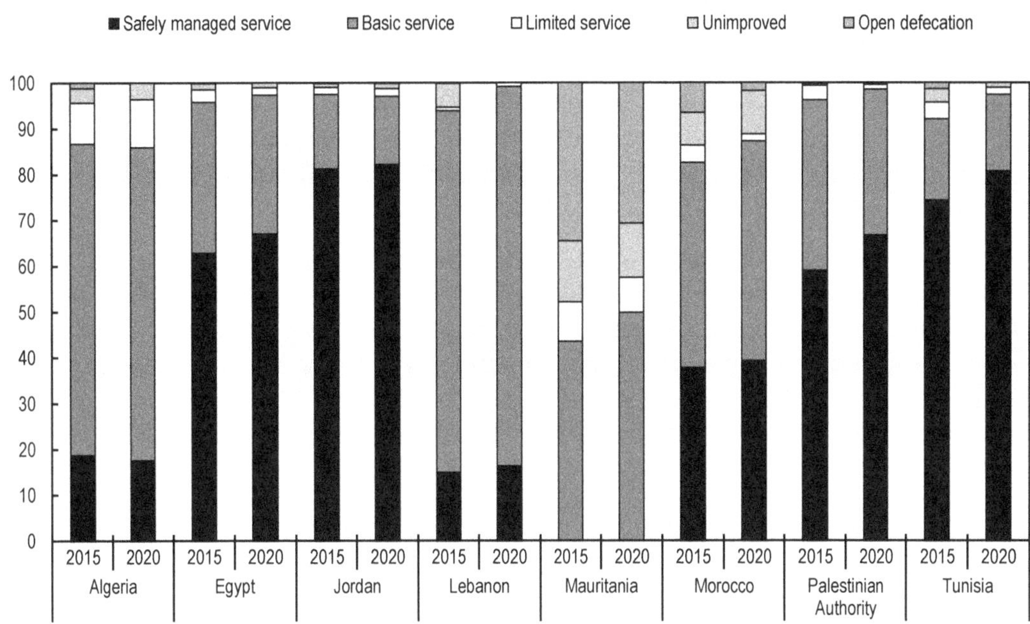

Source: World Health Organisation, https://washdata.org/data/household#!/dashboard/new.

About 64% (corresponding to 8.51 km³/year) of the region's wastewater is not treated or reused, losing a potential source of water for instance for agriculture and landscape irrigation, industrial processes and non-potable urban applications (World Bank, 2018[9]) (Figure 4.3).

Figure 4.3. Wastewater in the broad MENA region, prior to COVID-19

Wastewater volumes (km³/year)

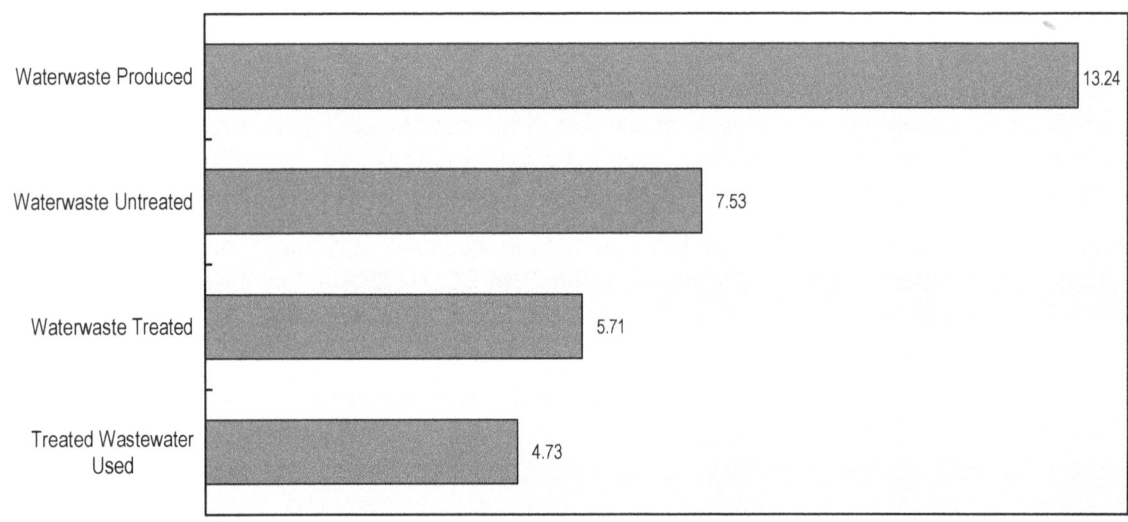

Source: (UNICEF, 2021[10]) https://www.unescwa.org/sites/default/files/event/materials/afsd2018-special-session3-presentation-omar-alhattab-unicef-en.pdf ; World Health Organisation, https://washdata.org/data/household#!/dashboard/new .

Water scarcity and lack of access to clean water and sanitation as well as poor waste management (including on hazardous waste, e.g. bio-medical and health-care waste) in MENA countries accentuated the impact of the pandemic. While data on water use and resources in times of COVID-19 are lacking for the MENA region, as data sets are foreseen to be updated in 2022, estimates of impacts on water usage range from an additional 9 to 12 litres of water used per day per person, an average increase of 5 percent for households, further straining water resources. Increased demand for water in the domestic households of the Arab region, which includes all MENA countries, accounts for an additional USD 150–250 million per month in domestic expenditures to satisfy additional water needs owing to COVID-19 (UN ESCWA, 2020[1]).

In coastal regions, the lack of or inefficient wastewater and sewerage infrastructure can impact the health and well-being of coastal communities. The development of new wastewater and sewerage infrastructure can create jobs while preventing future water-borne diseases, increasing water security and enhancing coastal water quality for tourism (World Resources Institute, 2020[11]). Infrastructure development should be accompanied by better water governance. For instance, the OECD report *Water Governance in Tunisia* recommended to strengthen stakeholder engagement and improve access to information, and to develop a complete database on water and sanitation services, including service quality indicators to bring greater transparency to the water sector (OECD, 2014[12]).

The COVID-19 pandemic emphasised the need for specialised employees in the water sector

Water demand in the region was growing at a rapid rate prior to the pandemic, driven by urbanisation, tourism development, irrigated agriculture and industrialisation. With increased water demand and a dwindling source thereof, securing and optimising the distribution of the water supply is becoming increasingly necessary. Increasing the efficiency of water supplies to ensure better water management in urban areas, productivity of agricultural water, improvement of the water-energy nexus, citizens' engagement and cooperation on cross-border waters will require new and reinforced human resources.

Despite these needs, the number of people employed in water supply and wastewater treatment facilities worldwide has consistently decreased, due to a lack of interest from new graduates in jobs in the water sector and a lack of resources to hire and retain skilled staff, especially in the public sector. It was estimated a few years ago that 3 out of 4 jobs globally are affected by access to water, where inadequate access can put extra pressure on workers' time and resources, potentially limiting economic growth and job creation, particularly in the coming decades (ILO, 2016[13]).

COVID-19 has marked a new era of work modalities as increasing digitalisation of enterprises capitalises on remote working capacities. However, some sectors in the broad MENA region, such as water systems, have been slow to reach modern technological standards and thus lack specialists that can operate complex digital tools in the water sector.

Lebanon is in urgent need of personnel that can operate water management systems such as Water Balance, the GIS system, SWMS and SCADA systems (UNESCO, 2020[14]). Specialists are also required to develop and manage call centres for water systems in Lebanon, as well as set-up and run e-payment modalities, but are few in numbers.

Meanwhile, skills associated with not only the digital aspect of the water sector (i.e. electronic technicians for control, automation, instrumentation and chemical technicians for water analysis, chemical dosing products), but also the mechanical side (i.e. plumbers, welders for steel and plastic pipes, fitters for special jointing like grooved for big pipes diameters, and electricians) are also currently missing from the workforce.

Policy considerations

- *Build up and support local value chains to lower agro-food import dependence and increase food security in the region.* The OECD's 3rd Roundtable on the Circular Economy in Cities and Regions discussed best pratice showing that companies with a higher level of circularity and local production faced significantly fewer challenges during the crisis than their linear counterparts did. The latter faced financial and supply chain-related problems, while the formers' flexibility, innovation and close collaboration with supply chain partners made it easier to navigate the crisis. The OECD Four Keys to resilient supply chains: Policy Tools for Preparedness and Responsiveness include a series of recommendations on anticipating and minimising the risks agains food supply chains (OECD, 2020[15]).
- *Conduct WASH needs assessments at local and municipal levels to identify areas where COVID-19 mitigation measures are most disrupted by the lack of sanitation.* This is particularly important for rural areas that do not receive high national attention and are therefore already overlooked when it comes to infrastructure improvements and funding allocation for sanitation services. While the highest burden of poor sanitation remains in rural areas, rural sanitation requires less investment to meet national targets (Coombes, Hickling and Radin, 2015[16]). In the context of COVID-19 mitigation and recovery measures, prioritising national investment in municipalities that are most affected by poor sanitation situations can be a strong method in deterring further spread of the pandemic, as well as avoiding further health issues and outbreaks.

As noted in the UfM Financial Strategy for Water, increasing revenues and allocations to the water sector to approach water financing strategically and optimise existing financial resources is key to addressing the region's need for funds (UfM, 2019[17]). In fact, benefit-cost ratios for investments in water and sanitation services can be as high as 7 to 1 in developing countries (OECD, 2011[18]). However, the broad MENA region has an investment gap in infrastructure that amounts to 7% of regional GDP to maintain and create new infrastructure over the next 5 years. While gaps exist in all sectors, cross-border infrastructure, road transport and energy sectors account for the largest ones with water and sanitation accounting for 5% of the funding gap (OECD, 2021[19]).

Although international investors and development agencies have become increasingly active in water infrastructure investments in developing countries, the need for more investment outweighs the current financing flows. Gaps between current and future funding needs can come from high initial capital investments with long-term waiting periods for payouts, high transaction costs due to small or context-specific project nature, and a lack of data to assess complex water-related investments (OECD, 2018[20]). Valuing water can also be challenging depending on the type of projects being undertaken, and clear plans on how revenues will be collected and used can be difficult to ensure for some countries facing changing conditions.

Investment in infrastructure projects in the MENA region plummeted due to COVID.

The UfM report on the role of PPPs in the financial sustainability of the water sector notes that the MENA countries are the priority members where implementation of the UfM Financial Strategy for Water is needed (UfM, 2019[17]). In addition, this report finds that COVID-19 has severely impacted greenfield investments, which are the dominant mode of entry of FDI in most of the MENA economies. OECD 2014 *Water Governance in Jordan* highlighted that in order to make private sector participation work for large capital projects in the water sector, a number of framework conditions are required to meet the upfront costs of investment and to transfer technical knowledge. These include: a strong regulatory framework, administrative capacity, financial sustainability and strategic planning of projects (OECD, 2014[21]).

The OECD estimates that capital expenditures on announced greenfield projects declined by 80% in the eight focus economies in the first half of 2020 compared to the first half of 2019, a significantly greater decrease than in emerging and developing economies as a whole (42%) and OECD countries (17%) (OECD, 2021[19]). However, although infrastructural investments decreased in comparison to previous years, new investments in the water and waste sectors are still being signed, albeit at a slower pace and mostly through development banks.

- In Egypt, a new project concerning the depollution of the Kitchener Drain in the Nile Delta Region via infrastructural improvements to domestic wastewater collection and treatment, solid waste management and rehabilitation of the drain infrastructure was signed in July of 2018.
- In Tunisia, the House of People's Representatives (ARP) has approved a loan of 295 million Tunisian dinars (over USD 107.3 million) from the Kuwait Fund for Arab Economic Development (KFAED). The National Water Supply Company (Sonede) will use the funding to provide drinking water in several cities across the country (https://www.afrik21.africa/en/tunisia-parliament-approves-107m-from-kfaed-for-drinking-water-in-urban-areas/).

Nature based solutions offer a cost-effective approach for water resource management and disaster risk to ensure a resilient post-COVID-19 recovery

COVID-19 emphasised the relationship between the well-being of ecosystems and communities. Nature based solutions can support green and resilient COVID-19 recoveries, as they allow for cost-effective infrastructural solutions, while simultaneously providing environmental, social and economic benefits and help build resilience (OECD, 2020[22]). These solutions are most often used for management of water quantity and quality, flood risks and coastal hazards, and have many long-term co-benefits, notably, human health, food and energy security and decreased coastal erosion. There are recent examples of nature based investment projects implemented in the MENA region.

- In Morocco, in partnership with GIZ, a project to protect genetic resources and retain their fair use has been ongoing since 2017 in response to over-utilised and increasingly threatened ecosystem services. The programme improves regulatory frameworks and municipal development plans, increases awareness raising and impact monitoring capacities as well as provides assistance in making use of biological resources. The project is expected to be applied in Algeria, Tunisia, Palestine, Egypt, Jordan, and Türkiye by 2022.
- In Tunisia, in partnership with GIZ, a regional programme for developing capacity for forest ecosystem-based adaption to climate change is tackling overexploitation of forests and impact of climate-related disasters on forests through connecting international actors with national forest management services and capacity-building. The project also has ties with Morocco, Algeria, Tunisia, Lebanon, and Türkiye.

Policy considerations

In order to aid in the UfM's constant efforts to ensure water security, protect the Mediterranean Sea and promote green and blue economies, further investment to update and optimise the region's limited water-related infrastructure and the prioritisation of water and environmentally-conscious policies are needed. To combat the impact of the pandemic, improve social and economic well-being and capitalise on the region's coastal assets policymakers should:

- *Increase investment in water-related projects and infrastructural improvements* on a local, national and regional level. As water supplies were severely impacted over the last two years and water continues to grow scarce, governments will have to invest heavily to both upgrade existing systems and build new solutions. Infrastructure projects to optimise water resources are needed such as large-scale water storage and recycling systems, flood control systems with an emphasis on water retention, sewage system upgrades, and desalination plants. A more modern approach to infrastructural improvements that combines supply and demand management is needed, especially in a region where 80% of water is consumed for agricultural purposes. In practice, this means increasing resource efficiency through a range of techniques such as including crop planning. The UfM has already identified Jordan, Lebanon and Tunisia as key areas for investment opportunities in the water and climate sectors in its report on *Identification of Water and Climate-Related Investment Opportunities* (UfM, 2021[23]). While the report highlights investments in water infrastructure, including for food-based investments, agricultural support can be an effective way to ensure both water and food security. Nation-wide or regional level farming irrigation improvements should be considered a priority for regional infrastructure projects as a large majority of water use is distributed to agricultural processes and would promote better allocation of water resources while ensuring a higher degree of food security for the region.

- Continue integrating nature based solutions into national policy frameworks to create an enabling environment that facilitate take up by both public and private agencies. These solutions offer a cost-effective alternative to grey-infrastructure investments that integrate social and environmental priorities into infrastructural changes. There is a need to combine grey, e.g. dams, seawalls, roads, pipes or water treatment plants, and green infrastructure, especially in the case of flood control. NbS can provide multi-faceted benefits to different policy areas at the same time such as water, climate, health, amenity, biodiversity.
- Design water investments along strategic investment pathways to consider how projects can be designed and sequenced to deliver resilient water systems over the long-term and under changing conditions (OECD, forthcoming). Lack of data and analyses makes it more difficult to secure investments for and manage infrastructure projects, hampering the ability of governments to progress water and sanitation infrastructure. The UfM report Toward a Sustainable Blue Economy in the Mediterranean region notes the need to increase data collection and evalutions on marine challenges like litter and pollution (UfM, 2021[24]).
- Strategically promote the role of intermediaries in sustainable water financing utilities for small scale water and sanitation service providers. In 2019, the first UfM Annual Conference on Water Investment and Financing (UfM, 2019[17]) discussed how to engage private financiers for water investments. A recent paper on the role of intermediaries to facilitate water-related investment highlights the need to shift from an opportunities approach to a more strategic one, which includes focusing on strengthening the enabling environment for investment (Lardoux de Pazzis and Muret, 2021[25]). Further, OECD work on blended finance for water and sanitation highlights how development finance can be used more strategically to crowd in commercial finance (OECD, 2019[26]). Recent OECD analysis in this area can be a useful reference for MENA countries, to aid governments in designing strategic approaches for the involvement of private investors in water infrastructure that avoid gaps, redundancies and misalignments (OECD, 2021[27]).

Sustainable blue economy

> *Initiatives to curb marine plastic pollution have begun to take form in the region, but the pandemic brought the progress of positive ecological impacts to a standstill*

Blue economies are known to support the preservation and regeneration of the marine environment and provide a valuable tool for positive ecological change (Sharafuddin and Madhavan, 2020[28]). However, blue economies require sustainable development approaches to coastal resource, a difficult objective given that the Mediterranean Sea collects 570 000 tons of plastic waste every year, accounting for approximately 7% of the plastic pollution from land to oceans and causing an estimated USD 770 million in economic losses to marine ecosystems and industries. The Maghreb and Mashreq regions in particular have high rates of plastic mismanagements, with more than half of plastic waste flowing into the sea (Acerbi et al., 2021[29]).

- Egypt is by far the highest contributor to macroplastic pollution from mismanaged waste into the Mediterranean sea with 74 031 tonnes per year, more than double the second highest macroplastic polluter, Italy, with 34 309 tonnes per year. Five of the top ten localities responsible for total water leakage into the Mediterranean Sea are in Egypt, i.e. Muntazah, Waraq, Umraniyya, Kafr Al-Dawwar and Al-Husayniya. This is partially due to the Nile's connection into the sea. Algeria and Tunisia also account for a significant portion of such pollution, ranking 4th and 6th highest macroplastic polluters into the Mediterranean respectively (Boucher and Billard, 2020[30]).

Moreover, due to its trends of circulation of currents, the Mediterranean sea's capacity to accumulate plastic pollution is high but its ability to release it is extremely low (Cozar Cabanas, 2020[31]). Aside from large plastic litter polluting beaches and harming wildlife, toxic microplastics and nanoplastics present a greater threat to marine life. However, with the exception of Egypt due to the runoff of the Nile river into the Mediterranean Sea, MENA countries remain low contributors of microplastic pollution into the sea (Boucher and Billard, 2020[30]).

MENA countries have begun to address marine plastic waste through national strategies:

- Morocco is developing a *Coastlines without Plastic* national strategy.
- Tunisia is identifying marine plastic pollution hotspots.
- The World Bank is supporting Egypt, Lebanon and the Palestinian Authority in developing programmes and activities to fight marine plastic pollution (Hasegawa, Acerbi and Anouar, 2021[32]).

Initiatives in the form of pilot programmes to limit the use of plastic and reduce plastic-related waste had already taken form in some of the region's countries; for instance:

- After Morocco banned the distribution of plastic bags in 2016, the government's marine litter projects enabled associations to produce and test durable carrier bags using recycled materials. It also allowed for the testing of a refund based system for plastic bottle and aluminium can collection for recycling circuits in an effort to prevent and minimise the use of plastics that pollute the Mediterranean in a way that could be replicated in other MENA countries.

However, initiatives to curb marine plastic pollution were hampered by increased need for single-use plastic coupled with ineffective waste collection systems. The MENA region is particularly stuck in the systematic failures of plastic value chains that do not hold producers accountable, generate high plastic waste, have limited collection and treatment capacities, and offer low profitability in the recycling sectors (WWF Mediterranean Marine Initiative, 2019[33]). Strengthening waste collection, recycling and disposal systems, such as through the introduction of extended producer responsibility, can increase recycling rates of plastics, halting the discharge of plastic debris into the ocean (OECD, 2020[34]).

Although microplastic pollution into the Mediterranean has many sources, most origins in the MENA countries' stem from waste mismanagement. Poorly managed wastewater and landfill infrastructure that is unable to keep up with rapidly growing populations is the main source of microplastics entering the marine environment in most of the region. For example:

- Tunisia's waste collection and transport has accounted for 75-100% of municipalities' solid waste management budget in some years, while separate collections for solid waste and plastic remain especially low.
- Lebanon faces a particular challenge when it comes to proper disposal of waste and plastics. Landfills are a chief contributor of microplastics into the Mediterranean, as with other MENA economies. Beirut's harbour is surrounded by three coastal landfills alone, one of which closed and two that are active but that reached their maximum capacities in July 2019 (Kazour et al., 2019[35]). Waste management infrastructure in the country was already lagging compared to other Mediterranean coastal countries prior to the pandemic, with the average composition of municipal

solid waste generated in Lebanon composed of 15% plastics, two to three times higher than France (El-Hoz, 2019[36]). The country has been further impacted by the massive explosion on 4 August 2020 at Beirut's port that killed more than 200 people and destroyed the landfill's composting and sorting plants. The volume of incoming waste, already compounded by increased single-use plastics for sanitary equipment due to COVID-19, increased at other landfills as sanitation services were forced to reroute to new destinations with decreased efficiency in sorting capacities, leading to further proliferation of marine litter.

*COVID-19 protocols provided temporary relief for the Mediterranean's **water and land environments fuel and air contaminants but pollution levels** are rebounding to pre-pandemic levels.*

Studies have shown that air quality (in the form of four primary air pollutants: CO2, CO, NOx, and CH4) in urban Mediterranean areas had improved in the periods where the strictest COVID-19 measures were introduced, with mean NOx levels during the lockdown period down by 32% compared to the same period in 2019 (Sifakis et al., 2021[37]). However, greenhouse gas emissions are rapidly reverting to pre-pandemic levels after the temporary decrease due to economic slowdown, leaving levels far from reduction targets (UNEP, 2021[38]).

The decrease in activity on the coasts from business closures and a decrease in visitors on beaches have also protected the marine environment from other forms of pollution such as plastics from beachgoers, hydrocarbon spillage, microbiological loads, and noise levels (Ormaza-Gonzalez, Castro-Rodas and Statham, 2021[39]). Coastal water quality has also seen improvement as water surface temperatures returned to normal at the height of the pandemic due to decreases in industrial discharge, as was the case in Tangier, Morocco (Cherif et al., 2020[40]).

However, while marine litter from coastal tourism and leisure goers decreased during the pandemic, the introduction of COVID-19 related personal protective equipment debris such as masks and gloves into the Mediterranean has become a new challenge. Not only were the products used as precautionary instruments in the fight against COVID-19 made of plastic, but they were also cost-effective and easily-produced on a mass-scale, allowing fiscally constrained countries to urgently acquire necessary protective equipment. Additionally, the initial decrease in oil prices, especially in the region, outpriced recycling and eco-friendly solutions, leading to further consumption and discarding of plastic-made products.

Rethinking subsidies and taxing methods to promote environmentally friendly practices can lead to greater sustainability of resources.

Environmental fiscal reforms through taxation and pricing measures offer the opportunity for MENA countries to raise fiscal revenues while furthering the environmental goals included in the UfM priority areas; for instance, eco-system conscious policies like taxing and charging for waste, water abstraction, water pollution and chemicals. This form of government intervention increases market incentives for firms and households to consider environmental damage when it comes to production and consumption methods, improving environmental outcomes in the long-term (OECD, 2017[41]).

Rebuilding MENA's coastal and maritime tourism in the wake of COVID-19 is an opportunity to integrate green and sustainable practices into tourism agendas

Making tourism businesses more sustainable benefits local communities and can create stronger linkages with the local economy, increasing local development potential. Coastal MENA economies should focus on policies and projects that support tourism *development* rather than tourism *growth*. Policies in the tourism sector historically prioritise growth, which relies on an increased number of arrivals or overnight stays that do not necessarily imply long-term economic prosperity, as is the case with tourism development (OECD, 2020[42]). Local and national tourism policies should be refocused on increasing local income and employment while considering development planning that take environmental benefits and capacity into account. Jordan has, for instance, took important steps into this direction by developing sector-level action plans for each of the green economy sectors, including tourism, within its Green Growth National Action Plan 2021-2025 (GGGI, 2020[43]).

Prior to COVID-19, some countries within the broad MENA region had already been active in moving towards greener models of tourism. Tunisia, for example, with the help of SwitchMed implemented several pilot programmes focusing on sustainable practices in ecotourism and the ecotourism business model. The projects aimed to provide advice on potential implementation measures related to energy, water and waste, as well as mentoring on the eco-labelling application process and fundraising opportunities for small and medium-sized tourist sites in the Southern Mediterranean region (UNIDO SwitchMed, 2018[44]).

Policy considerations

Fragile marine ecosystems that have been slowly recovering due to a lack of traffic during COVID-19 will continue to be adversely damaged without deterring incentives to stave off biodiversity destruction. MENA countries may consider the following actions to ensure a sustainable blue economy:

- Work with local and municipal governments to promote economic growth, employment, innovation and social well-being in blue cities. As most of the regions capital cities and densest cities are located on coasts, local governments are key players for ensuring that resilient, inclusive, sustainable and circular practices are used for city management. Blue economic activities such as tourism and fishing take place, create value and provide employment at the local level in these countries (OECD, 2021[45]). Cities have an important role to play, as they hold competences on sectors that are likely to have an impact on blue economies activities such as waste and land use, while water related investments in cities and responding to water risks are likely to affect how blue economy activities are carried out. Governments can look towards the OECD's principles on Water Governance on how to ensure effectiveness, efficiency, and trust and engagement (OECD, 2015[46]).
- Expand economic policy instruments for ocean conservation and its sustainable use, among other positive areas of environmental well-being and conservation. A range of financial instruments are mentioned throughout the UfM Financial Strategy for Water as a way to fund the water sector through public means. The Strategy can be usefully complemented by drawing upon the OECD PINE database (OECD, 2020[47]). The information collected in the database indicates that environmentally related taxes are the most effective policy tools to encourage environmental protection in OECD countries. Environmentally conscious taxes can cover a range of aggravated sectors for MENA countries, including energy products (e.g. vehicle fuels), motor vehicles and transport services, and measured or estimated emissions to air and water, ozone depleting substances, sources of water pollution, waste management and noise, as well as management of water, land, soil, forests, biodiversity, wildlife and fish stocks.
- Promote marine conservation by implementing environmental support that promotes biodiversity, for instance support for responsible small-scale fishers and sustainable management. MENA countries can also implement payments for ecosystem services (PES) to promote catch limits or quotas and use non-compliance penalties to disincentivise non-licensed activities.

References

Acerbi, M. et al. (2021), *Middle East and North Africa: Two opportunities for rebuilding after COVID-19 in green and inclusive ways*, https://blogs.worldbank.org/arabvoices/middle-east-north-africa-two-opportunities-rebuilding-after-covid-19-green-inclusive. [29]

Bank, W. (ed.) (2021), *MENA Has a Food Security Problem, But There Are Ways to Address It*, https://www.worldbank.org/en/news/opinion/2021/09/24/mena-has-a-food-security-problem-but-there-are-ways-to-address-it. [2]

Boucher, J. and G. Billard (2020), *The Mediterranean: Mare Plasticum*, https://portals.iucn.org/library/node/49124. [30]

Cherif, E. et al. (2020), "COVID-19 Pandemic Consequences on Coastal Water Quality Using WST Sentinel-3 Data: Case of Tangier, Morocco", *MDPI*, https://www.mdpi.com/2073-4441/12/9/2638. [40]

Coombes, Y., S. Hickling and M. Radin (2015), *Investment in Sanitation to Support Economic Growth in Africa: Recommendations to the African Ministers' Council on Water (AMCOW) and Ministers of Finance*, https://www.wsp.org/sites/wsp/files/publications/WSP-Investment-in-Sanitation-to-Support-Growth-Africa.pdf. [16]

Cozar Cabanas, A. (2020), *IEMed Mediterranean Yearbook 2020*, https://www.iemed.org/publication/mediterranean-medioplasticae-analysis-of-plastic-pollution-in-the-mediterranean-during-the-coronavirus-outbreak/. [31]

El Hattab, O. (2018), *Drinking Water & Sanitation in MENA and The SDGs*, https://www.unescwa.org/sites/default/files/event/materials/afsd2018-special-session3-presentation-omar-alhattab-unicef-en.pdf. [48]

El-Hoz, M. (2019), *A Qualitative–Quantitative Methodological Approach for Sustainable Reclamation of Open Dumps: The Case of the Controlled Dump of Tripoli*, https://link.springer.com/chapter/10.1007/978-981-13-2784-1_10. [36]

FAO (2020), *How is COVID-19 affecting the fisheries and aquaculture food systems*, FAO, https://www.fao.org/documents/card/en/c/ca8637en. [4]

GGGI (2020), *Jordan Green Growth National Actions Plans 2021-2025: Tourism sector*, https://gggi.org/report/jordan-green-growth-national-action-plans-2021-2025-tourism-sector/. [43]

Hasegawa, K., M. Acerbi and K. Anouar (2021), *MENA joins forces to stop marine plastic pollution*, https://blogs.worldbank.org/arabvoices/mena-joins-forces-stop-marine-plastic-pollution. [32]

ILO (2016), *Water drives job creation and economic growth, says new UN report*, https://www.ilo.org/global/about-the-ilo/newsroom/news/WCMS_462279/lang--en/index.htm. [13]

Kazour, M. et al. (2019), *Microplastics pollution along the Lebanese coast (Eastern Mediterranean Basin): Occurrence in surface water, sediments and biota samples*, https://doi.org/10.1016/j.scitotenv.2019.133933. [35]

Lardoux de Pazzis, A. and A. Muret (2021), *The role of intermediaries to facilitate water-related investment*, OECD Publishing, https://doi.org/10.1787/0d5a7748-en. [25]

OECD (2021), *Building Blue Cities*, https://www.oecd.org/water/regional/Flyer_OECD%20Blue%20Cities%20Project.pdf. [45]

OECD (2021), *Middle East and North Africa Investment Policy Perspectives*. [19]

OECD (2021), *The role of intermediaries to facilitate water-related investment*, https://doi.org/10.1787/19970900. [27]

OECD (2020), *Fisheries, aquaculture and COVID-19: Issues and policy responses*, https://www.oecd.org/coronavirus/policy-responses/fisheries-aquaculture-and-covid-19-issues-and-policy-responses-a2aa15de/. [5]

OECD (2020), *Food Supply Chains and COVID-19: Impacts and Policy Lessons*, https://read.oecd-ilibrary.org/view/?ref=134_134305-ybqvdf0kg9&title=Food-Supply-Chains-and-COVID-19-Impacts-and-policy-lessons. [15]

OECD (2020), *Nature-based solutions for adapting to water-related climate risks*, OECD Publishing, https://doi.org/10.1787/2257873d-en. [22]

OECD (2020), *OECD Tourism Trends and Policies*, https://doi.org/10.1787/6b47b985-en. [42]

OECD (2020), *OECD work in support of a sustainable ocean*, https://www.oecd.org/ocean/OECD-work-in-support-of-a-sustainable-ocean.pdf. [34]

OECD (2020), *Tracking Economic Instruments and Finance for Biodiversity*, https://www.oecd.org/environment/resources/tracking-economic-instruments-and-finance-for-biodiversity-2020.pdf. [47]

OECD (2019), *Making Blended Finance Work for Water and Sanitation: Unlocking Commercial Finance for SDG 6*, OECD Publishing, https://doi.org/10.1787/5efc8950-en. [26]

OECD (2018), *Financing Water: Investing in sustainable growth*, https://www.oecd.org/water/Policy-Paper-Financing-Water-Investing-in-Sustainable-Growth.pdf. [20]

OECD (2017), *Environmental Fiscal Reform: Progress, prospects and pitfalls*, OECD Publishing, https://www.oecd.org/tax/tax-policy/environmental-fiscal-reform-G7-environment-ministerial-meeting-june-2017.pdf. [41]

OECD (2015), *OECD Principles on Water Governance*, OECD Publishing, https://www.oecd.org/cfe/regionaldevelopment/OECD-Principles-on-Water-Governance-en.pdf. [46]

OECD (2014), *Water Governance in Jordan: Overcoming the Challenges to Private Sector Participation*, OECD Publishing, https://doi.org/10.1787/9789264213753-en. [21]

OECD (2014), *Water Governance in Tunisia: Overcoming the Challenges to Private Sector Participation*, OECD Publishing, https://doi.org/10.1787/9789264174337-en. [12]

OECD (2011), *Benefits of Investing in Water and Sanitation*, https://doi.org/10.1787/9789264100817-en. [18]

Ormaza-Gonzalez, F., D. Castro-Rodas and P. Statham (2021), “COVID-19 Impacts on Beaches and Coastal Water Pollution at Selected Sites in Ecuador, and Management Proposals Post-pandemic”, *Frontiers in Marine Science*, https://doi.org/10.3389/fmars.2021.669374. [39]

Prüss-Üstün, A. et al. (2008), *Safer Water, Better Health: Costs, benefits and sustainability of interventions to protect and promote health*, https://apps.who.int/iris/bitstream/handle/10665/43840/9789241596435_eng.pdf;jsessionid=DB4A0EF7C718EC96503579538E52A13D?sequence=1. [7]

Sadoff, C. and M. Smith (2020), *Water in the COVID-19 crisis: Response, recovery, and resilience*, https://reliefweb.int/report/world/water-covid-19-crisis-response-recovery-and-resilience. [8]

Sharafuddin, M. and M. Madhavan (2020), *Thematic Evolution of Blue Tourism: A Scientometric Analysis and Systematic Review*, https://doi.org/10.1177/0972150920966885. [28]

Sifakis, N. et al. (2021), *The impact of COVID-19 pandemic in Mediterranean urban air pollution and mobility*, https://doi.org/10.1080/15567036.2021.1895373. [37]

Soliman, F. (2021), "MENA Has a Food Security Problem, But There Are Ways to Address It", https://www.worldbank.org/en/news/opinion/2021/09/24/mena-has-a-food-security-problem-but-there-are-ways-to-address-it. [3]

UfM (2021), *Identification of Water and Climate-Related Investment Opportunities in Jordan, Lebanon and Tunisia*, https://ufmsecretariat.org/wp-content/uploads/2021/07/Invest-MENA.pdf. [23]

UfM (2021), *Towards a Sustainable Blue Economy in the Mediterranean region*, https://ufmsecretariat.org/wp-content/uploads/2021/07/21.7.19-2021UfM.studydefEN-web.pdf. [24]

UfM (2019), *UfM Financial Strategy for Water*, https://ufmsecretariat.org/wp-content/uploads/2019/04/UfM-Financial-Strategy-for-Water_for-web-paginas.pdf. [17]

UN ESCWA (2020), *The Impact of COVID-19 on the Water-Scarce Arab Region*, https://afsd-2021.unescwa.org/sdgs/pdf/covid-19/en/5-20-00150_covid-19_water-scarcity-en.pdf. [1]

UNCTAD (2020), *The COVID-19 Pandemic and the Blue Economy: New Challenges and Prospects for Recovery and Resilience*, https://unctad.org/system/files/official-document/ditctedinf2020d2_en.pdf. [6]

UNEP (2021), *COVID-19 caused only a temporary reduction in carbon emissions – UN report*, https://www.unep.org/news-and-stories/press-release/covid-19-caused-only-temporary-reduction-carbon-emissions-un-report. [38]

UNESCO (2020), *Skills in the Water sector in Lebanon: Overview of the needs after COVID-19*, https://en.unesco.org/news/skills-water-sector-lebanon-overview-needs-after-covid-19. [14]

UNICEF (2021), , https://www.unescwa.org/sites/default/files/event/materials/afsd2018-special-session3-presentation-omar-alhattab-unicef-en.pdf. [10]

UNIDO SwitchMed (2018), *Switching to the circular economy in the Mediterranean*, https://www.unido.org/sites/default/files/files/2020-01/SwitchMed-newspaper-Third%20edition.pdf. [44]

World Bank (2018), *Beyond Scarcity : Water Security in the Middle East and North Africa*, https://openknowledge.worldbank.org/bitstream/handle/10986/27659/9781464811449.pdf?sequence=14&isAllowed=y. [9]

World Resources Institute (2020), *Using the Ocean As a Tool for Global Economic Recovery*, https://www.wri.org/insights/using-ocean-tool-global-economic-recovery. [11]

WWF Mediterranean Marine Initiative (2019), *Stop the Flood of Plastic: How Mediterranean countries can save their sea*, https://awsassets.panda.org/downloads/a4_plastics_reg_low.pdf. [33]

Notes

[1] In this chapter, MENA region or MENA countries refer to the group of countries that are members of the Union for the Mediterranean. These countries are: Algeria, Egypt, Jordan, Lebanon, Mauritania, Morocco, Palestinian Authority and Tunisia. Where the term “broad MENA region” is used, it refers to the group of MENA countries that include UfM and non-UfM members.

5 Transport and urban development

In the MENA region, years of very rapid urbanisation and countries' inability to maintain a sufficient provision of adequate infrastructure and services exacerbated vulnerabilities during the COVID-19 pandemic. This chapter considers sustainable models for urban space and solutions to current vulnerabilities. It stresses the need to improve the governance of public transport in MENA countries, by shifting to a sustainable transport infrastructure, and to provide adequate finance to the public transport sector so that it remains affordable for users. The policy recommendations point to action to develop green and sustainable cities, aligning policies on housing, land-use management and transport.

Key takeaways

- The COVID-19 crisis has highlighted the importance of thinking about sustainable models for urban space and solutions to current vulnerabilities, such as distance to essential services and poor access to water. In the MENA region, vulnerabilities were indirect results of rapid urbanisation, one of the fastest growing in the world, which was not met at the same pace with sufficient provision of adequate infrastructure and services.
- The decrease in air pollutants in MENA countries during the periods of mobility restrictions invites a reflection on the health costs of increased pollution associated to current models of economic and urban development. Exposure to air pollution contributes to increased infections and eventually deaths from respiratory distress viruses, such as COVID-19. The region has a number of aggravating meteorological patterns (e.g. sandstorms, dust, heat waves and extreme temperature) increasing the danger posed by pollutants. Pollution reduction should be a priority while thinking about the future economic development.
- The pandemic fostered a reflexion on new solutions to urban congestion and urban mobility, to reimagine urban life and spark transformative changes in cities, giving rise to innovative forms of active urban micromobility, including non-motorised transport. The benefits of proximity were made evident during the pandemic, as social distancing and lockdowns naturally pushed confined populations to modify the scope of their activities. This has generated a renewed interest in neighbourhood life. More public and private initiatives on green and resilient urban mobility could be fostered to maintain the newfound habits and accompany a shift in habits.
- The pandemic also paved the way for reduced mobility through teleworking. Estimates of a scenario of, e.g., two days per week of teleworking - which would be equivalent to a 12.5% reduction in work-related travel - could potentially contribute to a 5% reduction in urban pollution and 4% reduction in NO2 pollution. These would require adequate policies on digitalisation in cities, making distant work a possibile option when jobs are almenable to telework.
- The crisis stressed the need to improve the governance of public transport, by shifting to sustainable transport infrastructure and providing adequate finance to the public transport sector so that it remains affordable for users. Affordable and accessible transport reduces the use of private cars, which represent the highest contributors to the increase in emissions in the transport sector worldwide. To develop green and sustainable cities, with enhanced access to services, it is important to align policies on housing, land-use management and transport, and secure proper financing for public transport.
- The global pandemic significantly slowed traffic in all modes of transport. While the long-term impact on transport services is still difficult to predict, there has been an acceleration in digitalisation within the transport and logistics sector, which can render the sector more efficient. The harmonisation of existing initiatives and strategies is necessary for a sustainable recovery, to reduce the existing gaps between the two shores of the Mediterranean by further developing the South-South and South-North interconnection, in all modes of transport.

According to recent estimates, cities are home to almost half (48%) of the global population and this share is projected to reach 55% by 2050 (OECD/European Commission, 2020[1]). The MENA region[1], in particular, has one of the fastest urbanisation rates in the world. Slightly lower than estimations for the EU-27 where 75% of the total population reside in urban areas, currently 60% of the Mediterranean region's inhabitants live in urban areas (Figure 5.1). This proportion is expected to increase by 22.5 million inhabitants within the next decade due to the broad MENA region's exceptionally high birth rates in the upper 20 births per 1000 capita, along with an upward trend of intensive migration from rural to urban areas (International Centre for Migration Policy Development (ICMPD), 2018[2]). These population movements are driven by a variety of factors, including the modernisation of the agricultural sector, alternative economic opportunities, and migration from countries in the region with political instability and ongoing conflicts.

Further estimates indicate that 28 of the 30 largest cities in the broad MENA region will experience rapid levels of growth, with populations expected to increase over 15% by 2035. The fastest growing cities (>35% growth) are expected to be Cairo, Tangier, and Alexandria. Moroccan cities are also projected to experience 30% population growth rates. Cities in Lebanon and Jordan are considered to be, comparatively, slower growing cities, albeit, they will still maintain an average of 10% annual growth (UN, 2018[3]).

Figure 5.1. Urban population in MENA and EU-27, 2019

As a % of total population

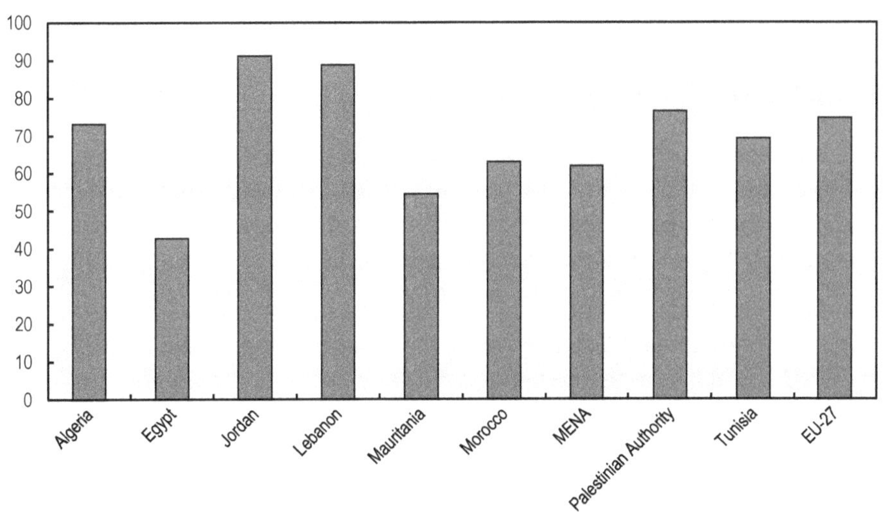

Note: Data for MENA include all MENA countries that are members of the UfM, plus Djibouti, Iran, Iraq, Syria and Yemen. Urban population refers to people living in urban areas as defined by national statistical offices.
Source: World Development Indicators, https://data.worldbank.org/; https://data.worldbank.org/indicator/SP.URB.TOTL.IN.ZS

With these high rates of growth in urban population, the region's cities face a range of challenges, all of which were exacerbated by the COVID-19 pandemic. Prior to the pandemic, the broad MENA region was facing growing urbanisation rates, but did not follow the same pace in creating adequate infrastructure and services. In consequence, the expansion of major urban centres in the Middle East and North Africa has outpaced the development of public service infrastructure, increasing the distances to public services. People living further away from urban centers are often not sufficiently connected to schools and hospitals and underdeveloped infrastructure leaves large part of populations without sufficient access to water, electricity and good connectivity to the internet.

During the pandemic, the containment measures not only further constrained access to those services, but also, in turn, inadequate access to basic infrastructure made it harder to contain the spread of COVID-19 and implement social distancing measures (Khavarian-Garmsir, 2020[4]). The pandemic especially affected vulnerable communities, living in poorer urban areas with poorer health, water, and sanitation facilities or refugee communities living in densely populated camps (OECD, 2020[5]).

Urban renewal, regeneration and development

The COVID-19 crisis has stressed the importance of reflecting about sustainable models for urban space and solutions against current vulnerabilities. Large-scale urban regeneration that densifies the urban core of a city is a complex, long-term process that requires great financial and political efforts (OECD, 2020[6]). Major adjustments to the existing urban fabric and urban networks, such as large-scale street furniture and public transport works, which are necessary in order to implement a sustainable urban policy are very often confronted with economic challenges and questioning public opinion. However, if they are carried out in a well-considered way, they promise not only to improve the sustainability and resilience of a city, but also to improve its liveability and strengthen its social fabric. This is particularly important in the broad MENA region, where cities are both critical to sustainable development and highly vulnerable to the effects of climate change. High levels of air pollution, which have previously saturated urban spaces, have experienced a substantive improvement during the COVID-19 mobility restrictions and confinements.

The global pandemic has created an opportunity by forcing a number of habit changes on urban dwellers around the world relevant to reducing pollution levels, such as shifting to biking and increased teleworking. It has also shown that more eco-friendly urban planning is possible by, for example, expanding non-motorised transit networks and infrastructure.

Air pollution in the MENA region

The question of the urbanisation of societies has always brought with it related issues such as the well-being of city dwellers, their health and living environment, the economic development of urban agglomerations and finally the correlation between these issues. The urgency and severity of the measures taken to stop the spread of the disease had an immediate indirect effect on reducing air pollution emissions.

Cities, which generate and attract a substantial part of the economic activity around the world, and engender a great number of motorised displacements, have become the areas where the main air quality problems happen (WHO, 2016[7]). Large cities are particularly impacted by air pollution, which adversely affects human health, ecosystems, agricultural productivity, the built environment, and the regional climate. Since 2010, air quality in cities around the world has tended to improve. There has been a reduction in PM2.5 concentration also in developing regions, with this positive trend being strongest in East Asia and the Pacific (falling by 4 percentage points) and in the Middle East and North Africa (falling by 5 percentage points (OECD, 2020[8]).

However, air pollution levels remain high in cities and tend to be higher in the poorest countries. In larger, cities, emissions associated with transport and energy contribute to high levels of localised pollution. The MENA region has a number of additional aggravating features, with large-scale (synoptic) weather patterns affecting pollutants. There are unusually high levels of ozone production in the region (Lelieveld, 2009[9]), because human pollution is mixed with dust, lifted into the atmosphere from deserts or local winds (such as the Shamal, Sirrocco or Harmattan). Dust (generally classified as PM10, or PM2.5 with particle diameters greater than 10 and 2.5 micrometres respectively) settles more rapidly in the atmosphere (Liu et al., 2009[10]). The larger particles are largely filtered by the upper respiratory system (nose and mouth), which is not the case for the finer particles such as PM2.5, which are particularly present in the MENA region (Figure 5.2). According to WHO research, PM, and PM2.5 in particular, are responsible for respiratory infections, lung diseases and, above all, a compromised immune system. Exposure to ozone, on the other hand, can induce oxidative stress leading to airway inflammation and increased respiratory morbidity, according to recent US studies.

Figure 5.2. Exposure to PM2.5 in MENA countries

µg/m3 annual mean, 2015-19

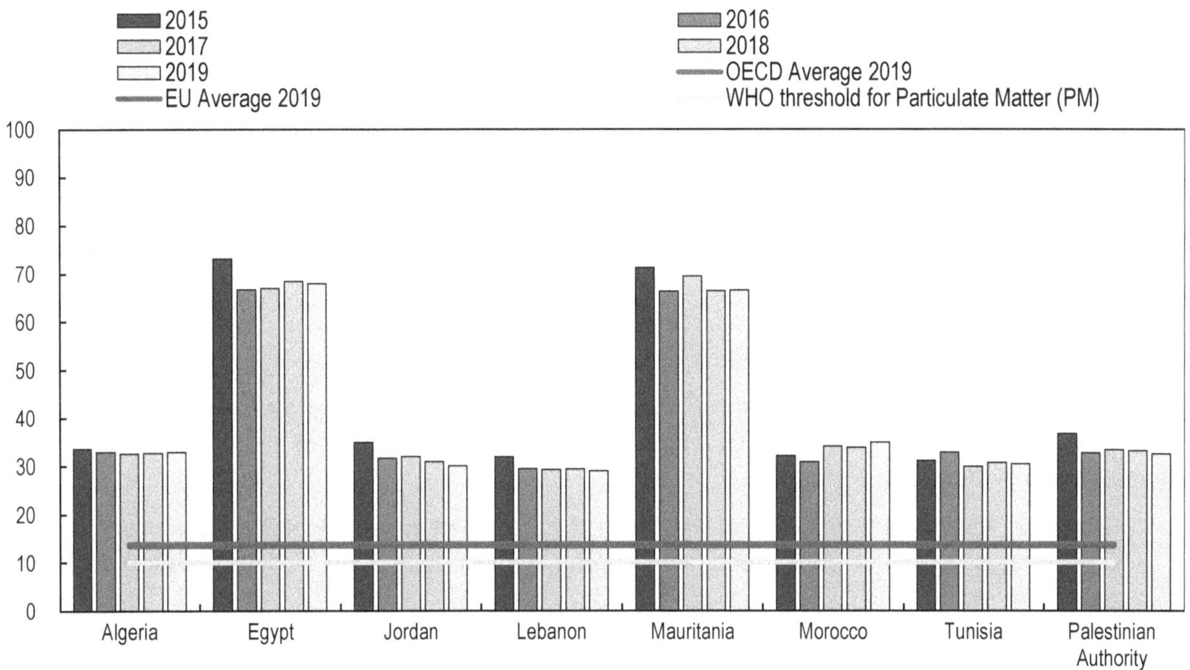

Note: The concentration estimates are population-weighted using gridded population datasets from the Joint Research Center Global Human Settlement project. PM is a common proxy indicator for air pollution. The current WHO threshold is that PM2.5 not exceed 10 µg/m3 annual mean, see: http://whqlibdoc.who.int/hq/2006/WHOSDEPHEOEH06.02_eng.pdf.
Source: OECD Stat 2021 https://stats.oecd.org/Index.aspx?DataSetCode=EXP_PM2_5# , Global Burden of Disease (GBD) 2019 project, Joint Research Center Global Human Settlement project.

Dust and sandstorms in the MENA region aggravate the impact of pollution on people's health, as both are in themselves factors of respiratory diseases such as asthma and act as vectors for toxic metals. In terms of the impact of pollution on viral pandemics, limited research has been conducted on the ability of dust to transport viruses, either short- or long-range, but it has been shown that microbes and viruses are more present in ambient air during dust storms. Findings also show that exposure to air pollution, particularly PM2.5 and NO2, contributes to increased infections and deaths from respiratory distress viruses, especially COVID-19 (Katoto et al., 2021[11]). While data on the correlation between COVID-19 deaths and ambient pollution in MENA countries are not available, pollution reduction should be integrated in any reflection on economic development of urban environments post-COVID-19.

Air pollution reduction during COVID-19 mobility restrictions and confinements. To fight the pandemic, MENA countries quickly implemented restrictive measures on the movement of populations with more or less severe confinements from mid-March 2020 onwards (Table 5.1).

Table 5.1. COVID-19 crisis and lockdown starting dates in the MENA region

	Date lockdown began	Type of lockdown (full / partial / none)
Algeria	24/03/2020	Full
Egypt	24/03/2020	Full
Jordan	21/03/2020	Full
Lebanon	16/03/2020	Full
Morocco	16/03/2020	Full
Palestinian Authority	05/03/2020	Full
Tunisia	20/03/2020	Full

Source: COVID-19 Lockdown dates by country | Kaggle; (OECD, 2020[5])

In the European Union, confinements coincided with a rapid drop in fine particle emissions; it was estimated that most cities reduced pollution levels by 30–50% compared with the same period in 2019 (European Environemental Agency, 2021[12]). Indeed, recent studies estimate that between 30 and 40% of pollution in urban areas comes from traffic-related emissions (Badia et al., 2021[13]).

Accurate data for MENA countries are not available. A series of local studies, albeit using various methodologies and sources, have shown a comparable trend in the decline of air pollutant emissions in the main cities of the region.

- **Algeria:** A significant reduction of PM2.5 (-11%) was seen in the city of Algiers when comparing the average values of PM2.5 recorded between January-June 2020 to those recoded during the same period in 2018-19 (Benchrif et al., 2021[14]).
- **Egypt:** PM2.5 concentrations were reduced by 46.3% during the full lockdown of April-May 2020 in Alexandria, when comparing to the pre-lockdown period of January-February 2020 (El-Sheekh and Hassan, 2020[15]), at the same time, NO2 emissions reached 15 and 33% of the emissions recorded in the same period one year prior in Cairo and Alexandria.
- For **Jordan** and **Lebanon**: A study conducted on 21 metropolitan cities in the larger Middle East and North Africa region measured pollutants such as SO_2, NO_2, and CO. The study assessed the impact of the pandemic lockdown of March-June 2020 compared to the same period in 2019. NO_2 concentrations in **Amman** and **Beirut** decreased by −56.6% and −43.4%, respectively, during the period of the lockdown (El Kenawy et al., 2021[16]).
- A similar trend was measured in **Moroccan cities**: In Salé city, during the lockdown measures, the obtained results showed that the difference between the concentrations recorded before and during the lockdown period were respectively 75%, 49% and 96% for PM10, SO2 and NO2 (Otmani et al., 2020[17]). PM2.5 emissions also dropped by -18 µg/m3 in Casablanca and -14 µg/m3 in Marrakech compared to the pre-quarantine period (Khomsi et al., 2020[18]).
- In **Tunisia**, PM2.5 concentrations in Tunis dropped by an average of 20% in March compared to January 2020. Similar trends were observed in other cities such as Sousse (7%) and Sfax (23%) (Chekir and Ben Salem, 2020[19]).

Increased teleworking as a tool for tackling air pollution and traffic congestion

Addressing traffic congestion by rethinking urban mobility after the pandemic. Since the pandemic started, teleworking or hybrid working has become part of the new urban normality. Several studies in the recent past indicated that telework can be a promising tool for urban planning and development, focusing on reducing traffic volume and improving air quality (Giovanis, 2018[20]).

Figures from Google Community Mobility Reports (Google, 2021[21]) observing movement of people during the COVID-19 confinements indicate that workplace attendance dropped by more than 60% in countries where strict lockdown measures imposed maximum teleworking, notably in EU Mediterranean countries such as France, Spain and Italy.

While there has been little analysis of the effects of large-scale telework on urban air improvement, it is estimated, however, that telework could potentially contribute to a 2.5-4% reduction of ambient pollutant emissions in cities. A study by the Institute of Environmental Science and Technology (ICTA-UAB) (Badia et al., 2021[13]) conducted in the city of Barcelona, highlighted lessons on air pollution reduction in large urban areas learned from successive lockdowns between 2020 and 2021. The researchers defined three different socio-occupational scenarios based on a two-, three- or four-day teleworking week, and studied the changes in pollution using an air quality model for each. The first scenario envisages teleworking two days a week. Estimates suggest that this would reduce motorised traffic emissions by 5% and NO2 levels by 4%. This scenario assumes a 12.5% reduction in work-related travel. A second scenario consisting of three days of teleworking would reduce pollutant emissions by 10% and NO2 levels by 8%, reducing work-related travel by 25%. A third, even more amitious scenario would reduce emissions by 15% and NO2 levels by 10%, if 40% of service sector employees teleworked four days a week, reducing their travel by 37.5%.

Teleworking might also represent a development opportunity for cities (UN Habitat, 2021[22]), particularly second-tier and smaller cities, the latter having the momentum to attract remote workers fleeing large city pollution and noise in favour of calmer urban areas. Those cities might become exponentially attractive by investing in services desired by high-tech remote workers: broadband, healthcare, with a focus on sustainability.

However, people and places are unequal to telework, and the MENA region faces vulnerabilities that could limit the feasibility of teleworking. In general, a global trend is that cities have a higher share of jobs suitable for telework (13% more than in rural areas). Secondly, infrastructure gaps or digital inequalities also come into play (OECD, 2020[8]). Many workers in the MENA region cannot benefit from teleworking opportunities, because of the nature of their job (e.g. manual) and/or or the digital divide present throughout the region.

- A large proportion of workers in the MENA region are in informal employment and are more likely to be exposed to health and safety risks without appropriate protection, such as masks or hand sanitisers. Moreover, many informal jobs cannot be performed by teleworking, e.g. construction and many activities in the services sector which produce a large part of the region's GDP.
- Moreover, many workers in the region do not have a stable broadband internet connection at home, and/or companies cannot afford to provide their employees with the technology to telework.

As cities move from emergency responses to long-term strategies, strengthening and expanding access to the internet and digital equipment becomes an important part of recovery and resilience.

A shift in urban mobility

In an attempt to prevent the initial spread of the coronavirus, early government responses included restricting non-essential travel, reducing transport services, and implementing rigorous hygiene and distancing measures on public transport. These regulations had a severe impact on the urban transport sector, which is still struggling worldwide with reduced passenger loads by 50-90% and revenue losses of up to 75% in 2021 (World Economic Forum, 2021[23]). Despite the remarkable ability of public transport systems in developed countries to limit transport-related COVID clusters, the recent experience of **reduced traffic and air pollution** has motivated many city leaders to pursue greener and more sustainable forms of urban mobility.

The pandemic encouraged the proliferation of non-motorised transport, such as bike and walking, triggered by both public action and individual responses. During the lockdowns, forms of micromobility such as walking in the neighbourhood has replaced cross-city travel while cycling is an effective alternative for longer trips previously taken by public transport (ITF, 2021[24]). These modes also took on more importance in some cities as private motor vehicle use was restricted or discouraged. In Amman and across much of the rest of Jordan, for instance, Cars were officially banned for 40 days in order to limit the distances travelled by Jordanians, thus creating a hybrid containment, which encouraged a shift to other means of transport to the exclusion of public transports. Other cities have made cycling a preferred option by deploying bicycle emergency lines, while others have created wider pavements by blocking sections of the curb.

Although this trend of alternative mobility started as a temporary measure, cities are already looking to permanently expand their non-motorised transit networks and infrastructure as a strategy to reduce personal vehicle use, decrease demand for congested public transport, all while improving local air quality and reducing CO2 emissions.

- In fact, retrofitting of streets into bike lanes became a recurring global trend in cities such as Berlin, Bogota, Kampala, Lima, Nairobi and New York. The mayor of Milan in Italy – home to one of the most polluted regions in Europe – has announced that the city will retrofit 22 miles of streets for post-COVID cycling and walking as a commitment towards micro and clean forms of urban mobility (UN Habitat, 2021[22]).

While each MENA member has its own specificities, there is a trend towards public and private initiatives to foster green and more resilient urban mobility.

- **Egypt:** The Ministry of Youth and Sports is launching the fourth round of '**Your Bike... Your Health**' initiative which offers all-new electric bikes at reduced prices to encourage youths to use bikes to improve lifestyle and fitness and change commuting habits. Egypt has a very limited amount of cycling tracks, but this is in process to change. The Government of the Netherlands and the GEF Small Grants Programme (SGP), as well as UNDP are working on various projects to encourage non-motorised transport, including the establishment of cycling lanes, student loans for buying bicycles, as well as pioneering a university bike-sharing scheme. This showcases the viability of cycle-sharing schemes in Egypt (UNDP, 2021[25]). The latter are also under private initiative scrutiny, such as the Tabdeel initiative to create cleaner, healthier and human-centred cities in Egypt and North Africa through redesigning urban infrastructures to promote bicycling. Tabdeel is currently working with governmental authorities to create Egypt's first legal code for designing streets that accommodate cycling (Wagner, 2021[26]).
- **Lebanon**: The current dire economic situation took a toll on car imports, with the latter falling by 70% over the past 2 years. Moreover, the monetary situation is currently creating shortages in fuel. As a result, non-motorised means of transport and carpooling are becoming the new transport norm. The cycling culture is rapidly growing in Lebanon and private initiatives for a more sustainable transport are the key; an example is Wave, a subscription-based service for renting electric bicycles launched by private Dutch investment in March 2021 (Kanaan, 2021[27]). Hadeer bus company, a local SME, which provides affordable bus transport along the country's northern coastal highway was created during the COVID-19 crisis and presents itself as an alternative to deficient public transport. Hadeer's services also aims to reconnect female populations as 60% of its customers are women (France24, 2021[28]). Beirut municipality is also promoting other means of transport such as tuk-tuks.
- **Jordan:** The country is on the forefront of the shift towards a more sustainable urban mobility. Following the outbreak of COVID-19 pandemic, the Mayor of Greater Amman Municipality (GAM) formed an emergency taskforce intended to enhance accessibility of critical urban services for citizens. Moreover, with the support of the EBRD, the Amman Green City Action Plan (GCAP) 2021 was put in place. Objectives include the increase in modal share of public transport by 30% by 2030, development of a strategy to support pedestrian travel, and incorporation of smart systems

in transporation planning (Greater Amman Municipality, EBRD, 2021[29]) (Greater Amman Municipality, 2020[30]) (Tarawneh et al., 2020[31]).

This trend follows a worldwide pattern: The pandemic has led to the rapid reorganisation of urban space, with for example, in some OECD countries, the occasional and sometimes sustained widening of pavements, pedestrianisation of streets and cycle lanes to meet the urgent need for social distancing. This global experiment in 'tactical urbanism' has proven to be a powerful tool for governments to reduce the dependence of urban spaces on the automobile (OECD, LSECities, 2021[32]). In the long-term, promoting innovative and sustainable policies related to urban space design as well as forms of active mobility, such as walking and cycling, compact, transit-oriented and mixed land-use and accessible and affordable public transport would be a comprehensive approach that addresses at the same time recovery post pandemic, climate change and inclusivity. In the MENA region, there are limitations that need to be first addressed, such as the prominence of car-centric urban development, negative socio-economic bias on cycling, insufficient technical resources to allot to sustainable transport, rugged topography, and high temperatures and humidity in the summer. Nonetheless, the adoption of mobility alternatives and reclaiming street spaces for pedestrians in the MENA countries can have multifaceted and widespread benefits. Moreover, as demonstrated in Egypt and Lebanon, private initiatives play an important role in the urban mobility transition.

Policy considerations

Municipalities in MENA countries could foster urban development, renewal and regeneration by drawing on the experience accumulated by cities in OECD countries in their responses to the pandemic. In many cases, the crisis acted as an accelerator of positive changes (OECD, 2020[6]), specially in the transport planning area (OECD, 2020[33]). MENA countries should also further build on the UfM Guidance Framework for Sustainable Euro-Mediterranean Cities and Territories (UfM, 2013[34]) and the UfM Urban Agenda (UfM, 2017[35]). The following recommendations could be considered:

- **Promote accessibility** to services. MENA countries should include measures in their recovery packages that also promote better accessibility. Improving public transport is essential, but should not be considered in isolation from housing and land-use planning.
- **Build green and smart cities** capable of moving to a low-carbon economy that promote better livelihoods and health of citizens. Smart cities initiatives leverage digitalisation to deliver more efficient, sustainable and inclusive urban services and boost citizens well-being (OECD, 2020[36]), (OECD, 2021[37]). Many cities in the OECD area are going beyond a technology supply-driven approach that used to prevail in the past and are adopting a human-centric approach to advance more sustainable urban development (OECD, 2021[38]). Public services such as real-time data, electronic city tolls, smart parking systems and an integrated smart network of electric-zero carbon transport options are examples of the way forward.
- **Promote net-zero carbon neighbourhoods** with green buildings and renewable energy; mixed land use which allows job-home proximity, incentivise inner-city/adjacent urban development (as opposed to suburban development); incentivise transit-oriented development. MENA countries could also look at examples in Tokyo, New York, Melbourne on how to transform central business districts (where offices are exclusively located) into mixed urban neighbourhoods with more housing, commercial functions.
- **Improving the quality and affordability of public transport,** via for instance integrated ticket system across modes of transport, and i**mprove the active mobility** (walking and cycling) as the last-mile connectivity, by creating dedicated spaces such as sidewalks, bike lanes and the necessary infrastructure for bicycle network. This involves also promoting local private initiatives in this direction, and appropriate regulation for the sharing economy.

- **Facilitate teleworking possibilities** as an opportunity for the development of municipalities and neighbourhoods in disadvantaged areas of MENA countries. The OECD has outlined guiding principles and policy recommendations for a smooth transition towards a sustainable teleworking model for people, places and firms (OECD, 2020[39]).
- **Promote national urban policies** that can provide municipalities with a long-term vision and mechanisms to vertical and horizontal coordination (OECD/UN-HABITAT/UNOPS, 2021[40]) and facilitate exchange and sharing between municipal actors and urban practioners of different cities, city-to-city partnerships between cities facing common challenges.

Social cohesion and reduction of socio-economic gaps

Providing equal opportunities and basic needs to all citizens, regardless of their backgrounds, religions, ethnicities and social status is an increasing challenge for city planners and policymakers, as inequalities are steadily rising and represent threats to the stability and security of societies. Urban planners have the crucial task of facilitating the interaction and social mixing in the community by delivering well-connected and liveable urban patterns.

The COVID-19 pandemic has aggravated existing socioeconomic vulnerabilities with a disproportionate impact on the world's most vulnerable and marginalised communities, such as migrants, the poor, women, and the elderly. Women, for instance, account for 70% of the world's health and social care workforce dependent on physical interaction; and as a result of lower-paid jobs, they are more prone to adverse economic and social impacts than male workers (OECD, 2020[6]) (OECD/European Commission, 2020[1]). Also, people with already limited access to basic services and essential needs were more severely hit by social distancing measures and closures, with those in the informal sector losing an average of 60% of their income at the outset of the pandemic (ITF, 2021[24]) (Chapter 1 and 3). Moreover, as more people spend the majority of time, during the COVID-19 introduced containment measures, indoors, people had limited exposure to green spaces and reduced opportunities for social engagement which limits opportunities for developing social cohesion.

The untapped potential to rethink urban planning to improve social cohesion should not be underestimated. In the context of the broad MENA region,

- Home to a large group of refugees from Syria, Iraq, and the Palestinian Authority, Amman faces challenges in maintaining social cohesion due to the lack of capacity to absorb this urban growth with unique ethnic mixtures (International Centre for Migration Policy Development (ICMPD), 2018[2]). The significant influx of migrants and refugees towards urban centres, for instance, has placed further pressure on local authorities' ability to adequately plan for sustainable urban development and provide efficient infrastructure, resulting in prominent socio-spatial divisions based on economic and wealth distribution.
- In Cairo, over two thirds of the city's population resides in informal areas, acting as a major barrier to Egypt's ability to deliver equitable social, economic, and environmental benefits to its residents (Jaad and Abdelghany, 2021[41]). The inability to control city growth can nurture various urban issues, e.g. formation of slums or informal settlements by urban centres, lack of infrastructure services (clean water, sewage, transport), and vulnerability to epidemic diseases.

Although population density (people per sq. km of land area) has been increasing by approximately 1.8% a year since 2015 (World Bank, 2020[42]), many cities have failed to capitalise on their population sizes and densities by not sufficiently investing in public transport systems and roads (FES, 2020[43]). Poor urban metro and bus networks increase the private use of cars, creating urban congestion. Density plays an important role in resource consumption, as it also increases the potential of other economies of scale, as for instance efficient heating and/or cooling of buildings, decreases the use of materials and the cost of infrastructure.

Changing use of public spaces as an opportunity for reimagining the neighbourhood for people

Urban spaces can be critical instruments in increasing social cohesion, yet they are often underutilised. The crucial need for this reignited emphasis on proximity was further made evident during the COVID-19 pandemic, as social distancing and restrictions on movement naturally pushed confined populations to reduce the scope of their activities, if they could. This has created a newfound emphasis on neighbourhood life and life in localised urban areas in general. The way city dwellers now use public space and local facilities has changed dramatically in many cities - and potentially in the long term.

In the MENA economies of the UfM, public spaces have been rapidly adapted to support emergency services through the provision of temporary hospitals, warehouses and other facilities that have helped to improve the response capacity of neighbourhoods.

Policy considerations

A lesson from the pandemic is that a new, long-term approach to urban planning should be envisaged to realise better and more equitable distribution and access to health services, while promoting healthy and active lifestyles. The potential increase in teleworking and the consequent reduction in travel needs, as well as the emergence of innovative urban mobility pathways, are likely to create a growing demand for local and easily accessible services and facilities. In order to improve social cohesion and the reduction of socio-economic gaps, MENA countries could consider the following recommendations:

- **Ensure equitable opportunities and services** by ensuring proximity between facilities, transport, places of employment and housing, accessible for all citizens from different social groups and different locations across the city. Moreover, there should be different affordable housing types for different social groups provided. The cost of living and housing affordability drives certain groups into different areas of cities. The transport infrastructure plays a crucial role, not only in how people commute, but also in what populations come into contact with each other in their daily lives.
- **Capitalise on common interests of residents living in certain areas of a or within a city.** Some identities and activities around entertainment, food and family are embraced universally. This could also take place in the spaces and moments between different activities, as spontaneous interactions are more likely to happen in these circumstances. This makes slightly congested, intensely used spaces, as markets, that overlap with novel activities the most conducive space for social cohesion.
- **Create urban green spaces as a tool to foster social cohesion**. Urban green spaces, referring to areas as gardens, parks, greenways and other areas with grass and trees, may support and positively influence the social fabric of urban areas in a variety of ways (Jennings and Bamkole, 2019[44]). Urban green spaces afford opportunities for people to get outdoors and interact with nature and others in ways that may not occur in other settings. Various health promoting behaviours in urban green spaces may cultivate social cohesion and vice versa. Nevertheless, the level of engagement within the green space can vary based upon qualities of the green space, the intended use, and an area's overall social context.
- **Shift to proactive planning that fosters resilience,** in order to respond to future scenarios. The traditional tasks of urban planners in managing land use to provide services and needs are no longer enough to cope with the complex and massive growth of cities. In a world that is constantly changing, a more adaptable and responsive approach is needed. This process should also facilitate **participatory approaches in city-planning**, which is crucial for fulfilling equality among

citizens, as participatory planning enhances people's sense of belonging and social inclusion of all members of society.

Multimodal transport network for people and trade

The broad MENA region spent between 3% and 5% of GDP annually in infrastructure in the last decade, mainly focusing on ports and airports. This spending was higher than in Latin America, Europe and Central Asia, but lower than in South Asia and East Asia. Important recent initiatives in the logistics sector were realised in Egypt, which has built the second line of the Suez Canal, and Morocco, which has significantly developed the Tangier Med port, enabling the creation of a modern trans-shipment centre, e.g. the Tangier Free Zone now covers 400 ha.

However, the region has seen a lack of investments in cross-border road and rail projects and the integration of transport infrastructure in the MENA region remains limited (OECD, 2021[45]). Also, despite the achievements, the quality and quantity of transport infrastructure in the MENA region still suffers from structural weaknesses (Figure 5.3). According to the Logistic Performance Index, Egypt ranked 60th of 167 countries in 2018, Jordan 76th, Morocco 87th, Tunisia 104th and Algeria 107th.

Figure 5.3. Logistics Performance Index in the MENA region, 2018

Score from 0 to 5 (best)

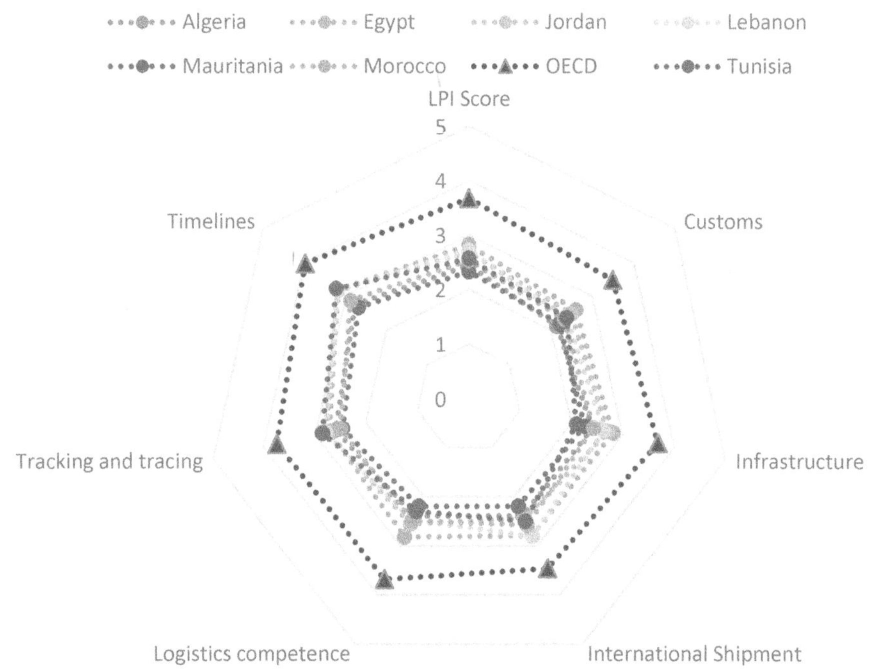

Note: LPI 2018 ranks countries on six dimensions of trade , covering customs performance, infrastructure quality, and timeliness of shipments. Data for the ranking are based on surveys of logistics professionals who are asked questions about the foreign countries in which they operate.
Source: World Bank, Logistics Performance Index, https://lpi.worldbank.org/

Face to the pre-existing deficiencies of the transport infrastructure, the impact of the pandemic containtment measures on transport and logistics varied across transport sectors.The disruptions due to the pandemic directly impact global supply chains and their underlying transport networks (OECD, 2021[46]). The closure of borders and the introduction of multiple safety restrictions and protocols limited the movement of people and goods. Between 4 and 11 June 2020 data for 97 land crossing points, 66 airports and 42 blue border crossing points, in the broad MENA region, indicate that around 65% of airports were fully closed and 30% were partially operational. 60% of land crossing points were closed, and only 37% partially operational. Furthermore, 60% of blue borders were closed and 33% remained partially operational (IOM, 2020[47]). The constrained transport activity also inhibited the delivery of essential goods in the broad MENA region to fight the pandemic, as for example medical equipment, personal protection gear and medicine (ESCWA; UNCTAD, 2020[48]). To ensure the arrival of essential goods, as medical equipment, trade facilitation measures were introduced by some countries.

The Covid-19 crisis did not stop **road freight transport**, even though some land borders were entirely closed. Some land borders remained open to carry essential goods, even to remote areas. However, road transport is estimated to have faced a 20% drop in activity during the various confinements in the broad MENA region in 2020 compared to 2019, which is equivalent to a loss of about EUR 22 billion. Overall, global losses for the goods road transport sector are expected to reach 347 billion USD in 2021. (IRU, 2021[49]). In order to further enable transport and trade, despite the confinement measures, many countries introduced safety measures such as changing trucks, sterilising goods, and imposing quarantine measures upon arrival (ESCWA; UNCTAD, 2020[48]).

For **maritime transport**, the number of calls by most types of vessel decreased considerably in the first half of 2020. The most significant decreases in vessel calls were for Roll in /Roll out (Ro-Ro) vessels (with a drop of 12.8%) and passenger vessels (with a drop of 18.3%). In the MENA region, Morocco experienced the largest drop in port calls with the pandemic, while Mauritania was the only country that recorded an increase, due to the rising number of tankers arriving in 2020. Maritime freight transport has shown some resilience despite vast adjustments introduced by ports and shipping companies, as the prioritisation of essential services and the reorganisation of operations and working conditions due to safety and sanitary protocols as well as a stronger reliance on digitalisation strategies (ESCWA; UNCTAD, 2020[48]). Within the third-quarter of 2019 and 2020, liner shipping connectivity improved compared to the same period in 2019, except for Kuwait, Lebanon, Mauritania, Syria, and Tunisia. Maritime transport further recovered during the second half of 2020 and into the first half of 2021. The rapid improvement of the maritime transport sector in many countries can be partially explained because of investments, including investments in dry-port projects that countries in the region are setting up, namely in Egypt and Jordan (OECD, 2021[45]).

The **air transport** sector was the most severely affected by the COVID-19 pandemic, as losses from movements of passengers impacted seriously the air transporters revenues. The number of passenger flights dropped by 53 % in the first six months of 2020 compared with the same period in 2019. According to the International Air Transport Association (IATA), international airline profitability averaged about $8 per passenger in the previous five years. Due to the COVID-19 pandemic, this has dropped to net losses of $73.2 per passenger in the Middle East (International Air Transport Association, 2021[50]). It is estimated that total revenue losses of airline companies in the Arab region are around $38 billion in 2020 (ESCWA; UNCTAD, 2020[48]). These developments severely impact MENA economies, as the aviation industry is of major importance, with three Maghrebian companies (Royal Morocco, Air Algérie and Tunisair) ranking among the 10 largest African companies.

Table 5.2. COVID-19 impact on air transport (2020 compared to 2019)

	Estimated impact on air traffic in 2020			Total Job losses in 2020 (million) estimations		
	Traffic capacity	Passenger	Revenue (USD)	Best-case	Baseline	Worst-case
Middle East	-60%	-132 million	-22 billion	-2.7	-3.4	-4.9
Africa	-58%	-78 million	-14 billion	-7.6	-10.9	-17.4
Europe	-58%	-769 million	-100 billion	-14.2	-18.4	-29.5

Source: (ICAO, 2021[51])

Globally, all airlines are confronted with liquidity issues and according to IATA, between 80 and 90 % of the world's aircraft fleet has not taken off due to the pandemic. Nevertheless, according to the IATA, Middle Eastern air carriers have witnessed a 6% increase in international cargo volume in August 2021 compared to August 2019, in order to compensate for the reduced cargo capacity usually provided by belly-holds of passenger air transport (ESCWA; UNCTAD, 2020[48]) (International Air Transport Association, 2021[52]). The pandemic is expected to have long-lasting implications on the aviation industry, with air travel not expected to return to 2019 levels before 2023 (ESCWA; UNCTAD, 2020[48]).

Transformation of the transport and logistics sector through digitalisation

New technologies are boosting e-logistics and enabling smarter trade, with greater efficiency throughout the supply chain and increased visibility and transparency, allowing the movement of goods to be optimised and redirected to where they are most needed. Digitalisation should become one of the pillars of resilience against future crises, as an essential tool to gain security, efficiency and modal integration.

- **Tunisia**, for example, has joined a UNECE eTIR pilot project to modernise its transport systems and facilitate the digitalisation of trade. Under a UN mandate, the IRU (World Road Transport Organisation) manages the TIR, the only global transit system and an important trade facilitation tool. Governed by the TIR Convention and operational in 60 countries, TIR provides customs guarantees, allowing goods to move easily, safely and reliably across borders. The IRU's eTIR system and the e-CMR digital waybill are two tools that have been widely recognised for their potential to support economies in the recovery from the COVID-19 crisis.

Before the pandemic, efforts to push the transport sector into the 4th industrial revolution were making steady progress. The COVID-19 crisis gave it a new momentum. As the digitisation of transport progresses, cooperation between governments will also naturally and mechanically become more important in order to effectively manage the huge amount of data produced.

The digitalisation of ports in particular seems to be a topic for the future in the post-Covid economic recovery and international cooperation in trade and transport. The digitisation and dematerialisation of port processes has been a crucial step in enabling the sector to meet the challenge of managing the pandemic.

- In **Morocco,** the pandemic crisis revealed the importance of the strategic choice of the Moroccan National Ports Agency to digitise port processes in 2008 through the implementation of PORTNET, which has become the single window for foreign trade procedures. During the crisis, the Moroccan port sector showed strong resilience and agility by adapting its various operational processes. Moroccan ports were the only border point that remained operational after the closure of airports and land borders during the lockdown.

Policy considerations

The disruption in trade and transport by the pandemic has highlighted the crucial need of keeping transport networks open, also in times of crisis, in order to deliver essential goods and to maintain trade flows. To leverage infrastructure and increase growth and competitiveness, and in order to recover from the pandemic, it is important for MENA countries to further develop multimodal transport networks for people and trade. Building on UfM's Regional Transport Acton Plan 2014-2020 (UfM, 2013[53]), policymakers could:

- **Promote digitalisation to support a sustainable and efficient transport and logistics sector,** build resilience and reduce emissions. Investing in resilient infrastructure yields substantial socio-economic benefits, as it reduces infrastructure disruptions, caused by natural hazards and poor maintenance. To this end, processes and procedures taking advantage of digitalisation and automation should be further enhanced. For instance, customs automation could be further promoted, as in Tunisia, by adopting contactless procedures in transport such as eTIR and eCMR. Moreover, single windows could be established which enable traders to communicate electronically with all agencies involved and fulfill trade related regulatory requirements.
- **Remove unnecessary regulatory obstacles to transport and trade** as well as to accelerate the post-pandemic recovery. Leverage trade and transport facilitation measures to ensure business continuity during disruption (ITF/OECD, 2020[54]).
- **Work to close or at least reduce the existing infrastructure gaps between the two shores of the Mediterranean**, through the development of the South-South interconnection as concerns land, air and maritime transport, as well as multimodal corridors. The private sector should be involved in the financing efforts to build affordable and resilient trasport and logistics infrastructure.

References

Badia, A. et al. (2021), "A take-home message from COVID-19 on urban air pollution reduction through mobility limitations and teleworking", *npj Urban Sustainability*, Vol. 1/1, https://doi.org/10.1038/s42949-021-00037-7. [13]

Benchrif, A. et al. (2021), "Air quality during three covid-19 lockdown phases: AQI, PM2.5 and NO2 assessment in cities with more than 1 million inhabitants", *Sustainable Cities and Society*, Vol. 74, p. 103170, https://doi.org/10.1016/j.scs.2021.103170. [14]

Chekir, N. and Y. Ben Salem (2020), "What is the relationship between the coronavirus crisis and air pollution in Tunisia?", *Euro-Mediterranean Journal for Environmental Integration*, Vol. 6/1, https://doi.org/10.1007/s41207-020-00189-5. [19]

El Kenawy, A. et al. (2021), "The impact of COVID-19 lockdowns on surface urban heat island changes and air-quality improvements across 21 major cities in the Middle East", *Environmental Pollution*, Vol. 288, p. 117802, https://doi.org/10.1016/j.envpol.2021.117802. [16]

El-Sheekh, M. and I. Hassan (2020), "Lockdowns and reduction of economic activities during the COVID-19 pandemic improved air quality in Alexandria, Egypt", *Environmental Monitoring and Assessment*, Vol. 193/1, https://doi.org/10.1007/s10661-020-08780-7. [15]

ESCWA; UNCTAD (2020), *COVID-19: Impact on Transport in the Arab Region*, https://www.unescwa.org/sites/default/files/pubs/pdf/impact-covid-19-transport-arab-region-english_0.pdf. [48]

European Environemental Agency (2021), *Monitoring Covid-19 impacts on air pollution*, https://www.eea.europa.eu/themes/air/air-quality-and-covid19/monitoring-covid-19-impacts-on. [12]

FES (2020), *Urbanization in the MENA region: A Benefit or a Curse?*, https://mena.fes.de/press/e/urbanization-in-the-mena-region-a-benefit-or-a-curse. [43]

France24 (2021), *Lebanon's car culture questioned in crisis*, https://www.france24.com/en/live-news/20211020-lebanon-s-car-culture-questioned-in-crisis. [28]

Giovanis, E. (2018), "The relationship between teleworking, traffic and air pollution", *Atmospheric Pollution Research*, Vol. 9/1, pp. 1-14, https://doi.org/10.1016/j.apr.2017.06.004. [20]

Google (2021), *Community Mobility Reports*, https://www.google.com/covid19/mobility/. [21]

Greater Amman Municipality (2020), *Amman's Urban Response to COVID-19 & Institutional Performance*, Greater Amman Municipality; International Growth Centre, https://www.theigc.org/wp-content/uploads/2020/11/IGC-Presentation-Amman.pdf. [30]

Greater Amman Municipality, EBRD (2021), "Amman Green City Action Plan", *Amman Green City Action Plan*, https://www.amman.jo/site_doc/AmmanGreen2021.pdf. [29]

ICAO (2021), *Effects of Novel Coronavirus (COVID-19) on Civil Aviation: Economic Impact Analysis*, https://www.icao.int/sustainability/Documents/COVID-19/ICAO%20COVID%202021%2010%2019%20Economic%20Impact%20TH%20Toru.pdf. [51]

International Air Transport Association (2021), *Air Cargo Up 7.7% in August Versus Pre-COVID Levels; Capacity Lagging Demand*, https://www.iata.org/en/pressroom/2021-releases/2021-09-29-01/. [52]

International Air Transport Association (2021), *World Air Transport Statistics*, https://www.iata.org/contentassets/a686ff624550453e8bf0c9b3f7f0ab26/wats-2021-mediakit.pdf. [50]

International Centre for Migration Policy Development (ICMPD) (2018), *City migration profile amman -executive summary*, https://www.icmpd.org/fileadmin/1_2018/MC2CM/City_Migration_Profile_Amman__EN.pdf. [2]

IOM (2020), *Tracking Mobility Impact - Points of Entry Analysis*, https://migration.iom.int/reports/middle-east-and-north-africa-%E2%80%94-tracking-mobility-impact-point-entry-analysis-11-june-2020 (accessed on 11 June 2020). [47]

IRU (2021), *COVID-19 Impacts on the Road Transport Industry*, https://www.itf-oecd.org/sites/default/files/docs/covid-19_impact_on_the_road_transport_industry_-_june_2021.pdf. [49]

ITF (2021), *ITF Transport Outlook 2021*, OECD Publishing, Paris, https://doi.org/10.1787/16826a30-en. [24]

ITF/OECD (2020), *Leveraging Digital Technology and Data for Human-centric Smart Cities*, https://www.itf-oecd.org/data-human-centric-cities-mobility-g20. [54]

Jaad, A. and K. Abdelghany (2021), "The story of five MENA cities: Urban growth prediction modeling using remote sensing and video analytics", *Cities*, Vol. 118, p. 103393, https://doi.org/10.1016/j.cities.2021.103393. [41]

Jennings, V. and O. Bamkole (2019), *The Relationship between Social Cohesion and*, p. 14, https://pdfs.semanticscholar.org/ca8a/96e9e854bfd58c5b5a7ae3314bf0ea518618.pdf?_ga=2.255490510.731937599.1636665034-235862595.1636665034. [44]

Kanaan, F. (2021), *Cycling culture gains ground in Lebanon as fuel runs dry*, AlJazeera, https://www.aljazeera.com/news/2021/6/24/cycling-culture-gains-ground-in-lebanon-amid-fuel-shortages. [27]

Katoto, P. et al. (2021), "Acute and chronic exposure to air pollution in relation with incidence, prevalence, severity and mortality of COVID-19: a rapid systematic review", *Environmental Health*, Vol. 20/1, https://doi.org/10.1186/s12940-021-00714-1. [11]

Khavarian-Garmsir, A. (2020), *The COVID-19 pandemic: Impacts on cities and major lessons for urban planning, design, and management*, ScienceDirect, p. 14, https://doi.org/10.1016/j.scitotenv.2020.142391. [4]

Khomsi, K. et al. (2020), "COVID-19 national lockdown in morocco: Impacts on air quality and public health", *One Health*, Vol. 11, p. 100200, https://doi.org/10.1016/j.onehlt.2020.100200. [18]

Lelieveld, J. (2009), *Air pollution and climate, in: The Physical Geography of the Mediterranean*. [9]

Liu, J. et al. (2009), "Analysis of the summertime buildup of tropospheric ozone abundances over the Middle East and North Africa as observed by the Tropospheric Emission Spectrometer instrument", *Journal of Geophysical Research*, Vol. 114/D5, https://doi.org/10.1029/2008jd010993. [10]

OECD (2021), "Global value chains: Efficiency and risks in the context of COVID-19", *Global value chains: Efficiency and risks in the context of COVID-19*, https://www.oecd.org/coronavirus/policy-responses/global-value-chains-efficiency-and-risks-in-the-context-of-covid-19-67c75fdc/. [46]

OECD (2021), "Measuring smart city performance in COVID-19 times: Lessons from Korea and OECD countries: Proceedings from the 2nd OECD Roundtable on Smart Cities and Inclusive Growth", *OECD Regional Development Papers*, No. 19, OECD Publishing, Paris, https://doi.org/10.1787/72a4e7db-en. [38]

OECD (2021), *OECD Principles on Urban Policy*, https://www.oecd.org/cfe/urban-principles.htm. [37]

OECD (2021), *Regional Integration in the Union for the Mediterranean: Progress Report*, OECD Publishing, Paris, https://doi.org/10.1787/325884b3-en. [45]

OECD (2020), "Exploring policy options on teleworking: Steering local economic and employment development in the time of remote work", *OECD Local Economic and Employment Development (LEED) Papers*, No. 2020/10, OECD Publishing, Paris, https://doi.org/10.1787/5738b561-en. [39]

OECD (2020), *Improving Transport Planning for Accessible Cities*, OECD Urban Studies, OECD Publishing, Paris, https://doi.org/10.1787/fcb2eae0-en. [33]

OECD (2020), *OECD Policy Responses to Coronavirus (COVID-19) : COVID-19 crisis in MENA countries*, https://www.oecd.org/coronavirus/policy-responses/covid-19-crisis-response-in-mena-countries-4b366396/. [5]

OECD (2020), *OECD Policy Responses to Coronavirus (COVID-19): Cities policy responses*, https://www.oecd.org/coronavirus/policy-responses/cities-policy-responses-fd1053ff/. [6]

OECD (2020), *OECD Regions and Cities at a Glance 2020*, OECD Publishing, Paris, https://doi.org/10.1787/959d5ba0-en. [8]

OECD (2020), *Smart Cities and Inclusive Growth*, https://www.oecd.org/cfe/cities/OECD_Policy_Paper_Smart_Cities_and_Inclusive_Growth.pdf. [36]

OECD, LSECities (2021), *Better Access to Urban Opportunities: Accessibility Policy for Cities in the 2020s*, https://www.lse.ac.uk/Cities/publications/research-reports/Better-Access-to-Urban-Opportunities-Accessibility-Policy-for-Cities-in-the-2020s. [32]

OECD/European Commission (2020), *Cities in the World: A New Perspective on Urbanisation*, OECD Urban Studies, OECD Publishing, Paris, https://doi.org/10.1787/d0efcbda-en. [1]

OECD/UN-HABITAT/UNOPS (2021), *Global State of National Urban Policy 2021: Achieving Sustainable Development Goals and Delivering Climate Action*, OECD Publishing, Paris, https://doi.org/10.1787/96eee083-en. [40]

Otmani, A. et al. (2020), "Impact of Covid-19 lockdown on PM10, SO2 and NO2 concentrations in Salé City (Morocco)", *Science of The Total Environment*, Vol. 735, p. 139541, https://doi.org/10.1016/j.scitotenv.2020.139541. [17]

Tarawneh, D. et al. (2020), *Urban Mobility and Spatial Justice of Amman*, Friedrich-Ebert-Stiftung Jordan & Iraq, http://library.fes.de/pdf-files/bueros/amman/18084.pdf. [31]

UfM (2017), *Union for the Mediterranean Urban Agenda*, https://ufmsecretariat.org/wp-content/uploads/2017/05/EN-FINAL-SUD-Ministerial-declaration.pdf. [35]

UfM (2013), "Regional Transport Action Plan for the Mediterranean Region (2014-2020)", *Regional Transport Action Plan for the Mediterranean Region (2014-2020)*, https://ufmsecretariat.org/wp-content/uploads/2013/11/UfM-Priority-Guidelines_2014-2020_EN.pdf. [53]

UfM (2013), *UfM Guidance Framework for Sustainable Euro-Mediterranean Cities and Territories*, https://inta-aivn.org/images/cc/Transmed/Background%20Documents/Guidance_Framework_April_2013_EN.pdf. [34]

UN (2018), *2018 Revision of World Urbanization Prospects*, https://www.un.org/development/desa/en/news/population/2018-world-urbanization-prospects.html. [3]

UN Habitat (2021), *Cities and Pandemics: Towards a More Just, Green and Healthy Future*, https://unhabitat.org/sites/default/files/2021/03/cities_and_pandemics-towards_a_more_just_green_and_healthy_future_un-habitat_2021.pdf. [22]

UNDP (2021), *All roads lead...to sustainable transport*, https://undp.medium.com/all-roads-lead-to-sustainable-transport-bac69012f71f. [25]

Wagner, A. (2021), *How Tabdeel is Empowering Young Egyptian Women One Bicycle at a Time*, Egyptian Streets, https://egyptianstreets.com/2021/10/06/how-tabdeel-is-empowering-young-egyptian-women-one-bicycle-at-a-time/. [26]

WHO (2016), *Health as the pulse of the new urban agenda: United Nations conference on housing and sustainable urban development*, https://apps.who.int/iris/handle/10665/250367. [7]

World Bank (2020), *Population density (people per sq. km of land area) - Middle East & North Africa*, https://data.worldbank.org/indicator/EN.POP.DNST?end=2020&locations=ZQ&start=1961&view=chart. [42]

World Economic Forum (2021), *3 ways sustainable transport can prolong the COVID-19 effect on air pollution*, https://www.weforum.org/agenda/2020/08/sustainable-transport-covid-19-air-pollution. [23]

Notes

[1] In this chapter, MENA region or MENA countries refer to the group of countries that are members of the Union for the Mediterranean. These countries are: Algeria, Egypt, Jordan, Lebanon, Mauritania, Morocco, Palestinian Authority and Tunisia. Where the term "broad MENA region" is used, it refers to the group of MENA countries that include UfM and non-UfM members.

6 Energy and climate action

This chapter examines national renewable energy targets of MENA economies in light of the COVID-19 crisis and their overall impact on the energy sector. It argues that the postponement of renewable energy projects, due to the prioritisation of immediate economic recovery, is counterproductive given the severe effects of climate change and the potential of an ambitious renewable energy strategy for job creation in the MENA region.

Key takeaways

- In recent years, the ambition level of national renewable energy targets of some MENA economies have steadily been increasing to reach more than 50% in total generation of electricity. The MENA region has also joined the global energy transition move, going beyond efficiency and renewables to include new technologies like green hydrogen, as is the case in Morocco, and electrification with renewable power such as electric vehicles.
- Fluctuations in regional oil prices due to COVID-19 have an impact on the attractiveness of green energy solutions in the MENA countries. In the initial period of the COVID-19 crisis, the impact of falling oil prices on the development of renewable energies was double-edged: while falling hydrocarbon revenues may have pushed oil exporters in the MENA region to diversify their energy investments, the same fall in price may have had the opposite effect on importing countries if the short-term cost of renewable energies and energy efficiency solutions becomes less attractive.
- Financial and priority constraints in the face of COVID-19 halted or ended some ongoing renewable energy projects in the region. Despite the MENA region being ambitious in terms of energy transition, the pandemic exacerbated the region's difficulties in getting renewable projects off the ground. Nevertheless, postponement of renewable energy projects due to the prioritisation of immediate economic recovery is counterproductive given the potential of an ambitious renewable energy strategy in terms of jobs is high.
- Oil market volatility due to the pandemic has highlighted the need to move towards renewable energy resources that can provide a stable and resilient source of energy for the MENA region. The need for public-private partnerships in the climate and energy sectors is therefore greater than ever. COVID-19 has exacerbated the challenges facing the region's energy infrastructure, with volatile growth and macroeconomic conditions, supply disruptions and the need to change operations to align with social policies and social safety nets. In this context, PPPs can help MENA countries to mobilise private sector financing needed to build resilience in energy infrastructure systems.
- The economic downturn caused by COVID-19, while slowing degradation for a time, has not fully prevented biodiversity loss. As biodiversity loss can be a driver of infectious diseases, the pandemic has proven the need for regional coordination for biodiversity. Increasing the comprehensiveness and alignment of national policies before tackling regional programmes is a first step. Enhancing coordination at local and national levels will be essential to avoid overlapping or conflicting policy objectives, which will help streamline regional efforts in the long-term.

Moving towards energy efficiency solutions in the MENA region[1] has become increasingly important for long-term economic growth and environmental wellbeing. The MENA economies have become more active in developing national energy efficiency strategies over the last decade, with most renewable energy targets and strategies spanning until 2030. Renewable energy targets have been set in the MENA countries, with some economies foreseeing ambitious targets of 50% renewable capacity, in line with some European countries (Table 6.1).

Table 6.1. Selected MENA installed renewable capacity and targets

Country	Installed renewable capacity	Current renewable electricity capacity (2020)	Target renewable capacity
Morocco	2 728 MW	33%	52% by 2030
Algeria	536 MW	3%	27% by 2030
Tunisia	324 MW	6%	30% by 2030
Egypt	3 660 MW	10%	42% by 2035
Jordan	2 400 MW	21%	31%
Lebanon	350 MW	2000 MW	30% by 2030
Mauritania	350 MW	21	41% by 2030

Notes: Morocco : although the official target remains 52%, sources report that teh countries will soon raise its renewable energy target to more than 64% by 2030 (Le Matin Maroc, 2021[1]) ; Jordan : data on current renewable capacity and targets was sourced from the National Energy Strategy 2020-2030.
Source: (IRENA, 2020[2]) https://www.irena.org/mena; (Ministry of Energy and Mineral Resources of Jordan, 2020[3]) https://www.memr.gov.jo/EBV4.0/Root_Storage/AR/EB_Info_Page/Strategy2020.pdf

Several MENA countries have also taken action to strengthen climate mitigation efforts, covering areas listed under the Plan Bleu's State of the Environment and Development in the Mediterranean (UNEP/MAP and Plan Bleu, 2020[4]). The actions of selected MENA countries shown in Table 6.2 are generally on par with neighboring UfM countries such as Israel and Türkiye (UfM, 2020[5]).

Table 6.2. Selected MENA climate adaption actions (2020)

	Climate change issues to adapt to	Adaptation actions
Lebanon	• Air temperature • Rain • Sea level rise • Sea water acidification • Sea water temperature • Droughts • Forest fires • Extreme storms • Desertification • Health hazards	• Climate smart agriculture • Enhance carbon sinks • Develop sustainable water services • Sustainable management of terrestrial and marine biodiversity • Reduce the vulnerability to climate change impacts of coastal zones, especially in cities • Ensure public health and safety through climate resilient health systems • Reduce disaster risk and minimise damages by mitigating and adapting to climate related natural hazards and extreme weather • Net zero vision by 2050 (target under discussion)
Morocco	• Air temperature • Rain • Sea water temperature • Droughts	• Program of reforestation 2010 - 2030 • Olive oil program 2020 - 2030 • Cactus planting project 2020 – 2030
Palestinian Authority	• Air temperature • Rain • Sea level rise • Droughts • Floods • Frost • Heat waves	• Mitigation cobenefits for planned adaption actions of highly vulnerable sectors, agriculture, Waste, Food, Energy, Water Health, Industry, terrestrial ecosystem, tourism, and urban infrastructure
Tunisia	• Rain • Sea level rise • Droughts	• Infrastructure • Land management

Source: adapted from (UfM, 2020[5]) https://ufmsecretariat.org/wp-content/uploads/2021/01/Enhancement-of-NDCs-in-the-SEMed-Region_WEB.pdf; (Energy and Climate Intelligence Unit, 2021[6]), https://eciu.net/netzerotracker.

Transition to green and cirular economy

Further fluctuations in regional oil prices due to COVID-19 have lessened the attractiveness of green energy solutions in the MENA countries

At the beginning of the pandemic, the economic shock in the MENA region was magnified by the collapse of oil commodity markets and capital flight from emerging markets. With the sudden drop in oil prices in March 2020, due to a decrease in global demand and coordination problems, the price of crude oil in the region experienced enormous fluctuations, adding to difficulties in planning of trade and economic recovery packages (Dabrowski and Dominguez-Jimenez, 2021[7]).

Fluctuating oil prices in the region play a large role in the attractiveness of renewable energy investments for MENA countries, as well as the broad MENA region as a whole, but in very different ways. MENA countries are mostly oil importing countries, whereas the broad MENA region includes GCC economies that are high oil exporting countries. Decreasing oil prices may encourage oil exporters to invest in sustainable and reliable energy solutions. For oil importing countries this makes transitions to green energy less attractive for governments and investors (IEA, 2020[8]). Major oil exporting countries in the region like Saudi Arabia, the UAE and Kuwait are already implementing substantial economic diversification plans to move away from hydrocarbons as an energy source due to the increasing volatility of the oil market (Hussein, 2020[9]). However, due to lower levels of FDI and tourism from oil exporters, there is a negative impact of decreasing oil prices also on oil importers, creating an opportunity for accelerated diversification and transition during recovery, making green stimulus from governments paramount (World Bank, 2021) (Bianchi, 2020[10]).

Despite the high potential of renewable energy for electricity generation, the share of renewables in the electricity capacity of the Southern Mediterranean countries of the UfM remains low compared to global trends, and also varies greatly within the region. It is estimated that the share of renewable energy in final energy consumption accounts for 0.1% in Algeria, between 5 and 5.5% in Egypt and Jordan, and between 10 and 12% in Morocco and Tunisia (Figure 6.1) (OECD, 2021[11]).

Figure 6.1. Renewable energy consumption

% of total final energy consumption

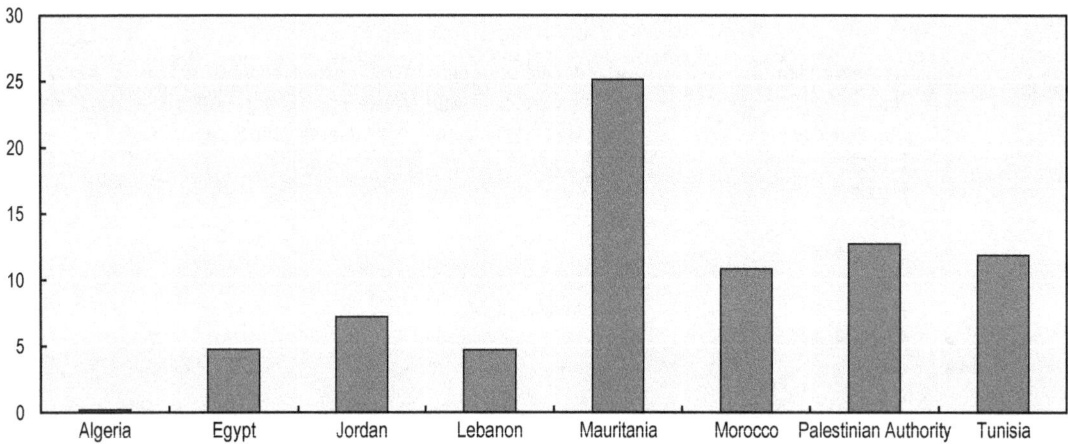

Note: Renewable energy consumption is the share of renewable energy in total final energy consumption. This indicator includes energy consumption from all renewable resources: hydro, solid biofuels, wind, solar, liquid biofuels, biogas, geothermal, marine and waste.
Source: (World Bank, 2018[12]) https://data.worldbank.org/

Financial and priority constraints in the face of COVID-19 halted or ended some ongoing renewable energy projects in the region

As noted in the UfM SEMed Private Renewable Energy Framework, the MENA region has seen some promising changes in moving towards renewables, such as the establishment of the Moroccan Khalladi Wind Farm in 2015 and the Egyptian Global Energy solar farm in 2020 (UfM, 2021[13]). Algeria and Egypt's solar plants have seen significant development in recent years, with Egypt having the largest solar farm in the world with further developments planned and Algeria launching a call for investors for a mega project in the solar sector.

There have been promising developments for the greater MENA region with respect to wind energy in particular, increasing from 286 MW in 2015 to 915 MW in 2020, with Jordan alone presenting an increase of 397 MW from 2015 to 2020 (IRENA, 2021[14]). According to IRENA's Renewable Energy Capacity Statistics 2021, Morocco is ranks just behind Spain and the United States when it comes to total installed capacity of concentrated solar power (CSP) at 530 MW. The region is also excelling with regards to total installed capacity of solar photovoltaic. According to the same report, Jordan and Israel rank the second and third highest in the Middle East region at 1359 MW and 1190 MW capacity respectively and Egypt ranking second in African region at 1673 MW capacity (IRENA, 2021[14]). However, OECD analysis finds that in recent years, the region continues to face difficulties in getting renewable projects off the ground, a problem which is exacerbated by the pandemic. Existing challenges to infrastructural projects included long and complex contractual processes, unstable political and economic landscapes, commercial bank deleveraging and tightened bank prudential regulations (OECD, 2014[15]). Ongoing planned renewable energy projects in the broad MENA region during the COVID-19 period reached a cost of USD 82.4 billion, only USD 4.1 billion worth of which are currently at an advanced stage of design or implementation. The other approximate USD 78.3 billion worth of planned projects have been decelerated, many of which are projected to fall through or heavily change in scope (Global Data, 2021[16]).

In the broad MENA region, large-scale infrastructure projects have already fallen through due to COVID-19, as was the case with the abolishment of the Kuwaiti Al-Dabdaba solar plant project which was anticipated to replace 15% of electrical energy needs in the oil sector. The heavy fluctuation and uncertainty of oil prices in the region, a principal source of GDP, and financial markets, are a key factor in these failures. Some MENA countries have also followed trend, with COVID-19 negatively affecting ongoing energy-efficiency infrastructure projects.

- Algeria has approximately USD 42.1 billion planned renewables projects in progress – the region's biggest pipeline - but around USD 41.9 billion of those projects have not yet been implemented or come to light (Global Data, 2021[16]).

The cost of postponing renewable energy related projects due to the prioritisation of immediate economic recovery is counterproductive to long-term economic growth. Countries of the broad MENA region already lag behind European and worldwide counterparts in terms of jobs in the renewables sectors, with a total of only 23 000 people working in renewable energy, notably in North Africa. Nevertheless, **the potential of an ambitious renewable energy strategy in terms of jobs is high.** In 2020, the renewable energy sector directly and indirectly accounted for approximately 12 million jobs worldwide (IRENA, 2021[17]). In 2021, the ILO reported that solar photovoltaics and bioenergy continued to dominate global renewable energy employment growth, accounting for a total of approximately 4 million and 3.5 million jobs respectively (ILO, 2021[18]).

Figure 6.2. Global renewable energy worldwide employment by technology, 2012-20

Million jobs

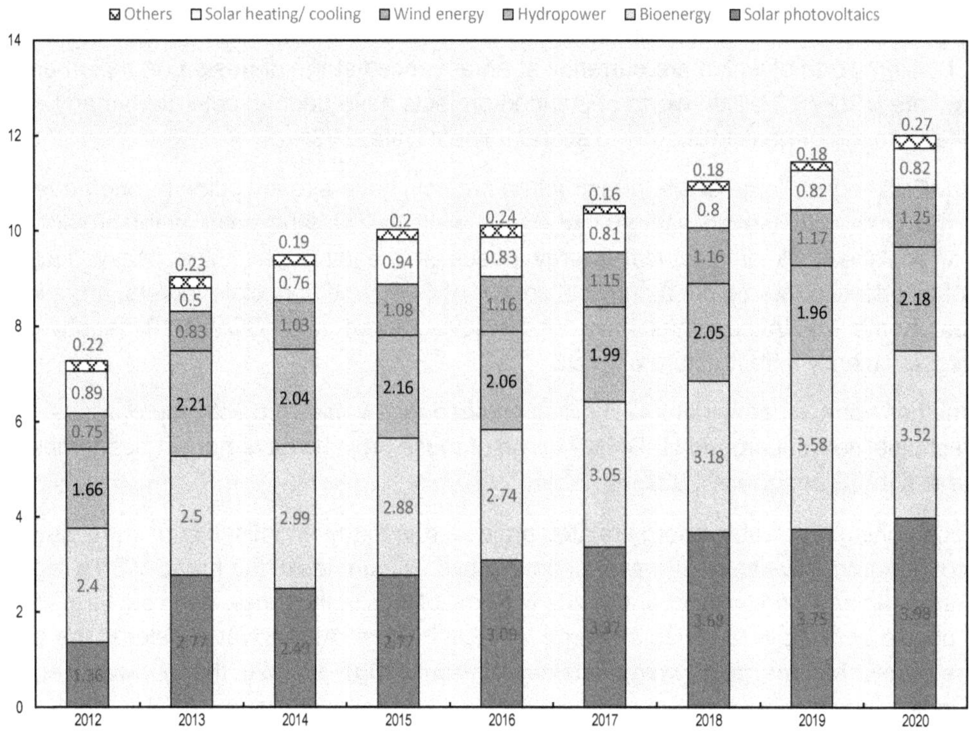

Note: Bioenergy: includes liquid bofuels, solid biomass and biogas; Hydropower: direct jobs only; Others: include geothermal energy, concentrated solar power, heat pumps (ground based), municipal and industrial waste, and ocean energy.
Source: (IRENA, 2020[19]) https://www.irena.org/Statistics/View-Data-by-Topic/Benefits/Renewable-Energy-Employment-by-Country

Figure 6.3. Renewable energy employment, selected countries and regions, 2020

Thousand jobs

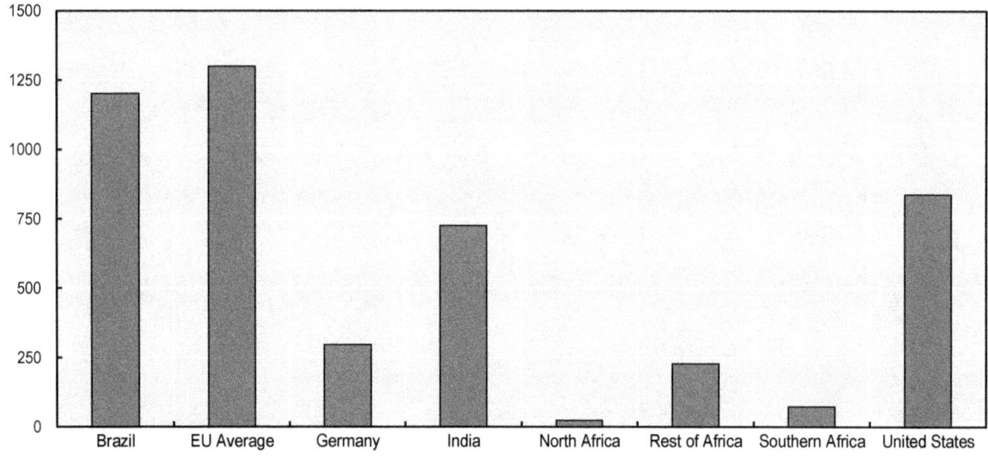

Source: (IRENA, 2020[19]) https://www.irena.org/Statistics/View-Data-by-Topic/Benefits/Renewable-Energy-Employment-by-Country

In MENA the total amount of employees in the renewables sector remains low, but is increasing. In Jordan, for instance, there have been promising develoments: IRENA and ILO estimate that the economy provides more than 6 000 jobs in energy efficiency (lighting and buildings), for a combined 11 300 jobs solely in Jordan. However, women held only about 5% of the jobs (8% in solar and only 1% in wind) (RCREEE and GWS, 2010[20]). The country employed approximately 5 000 people in renewable energy in 2020, comprising more than 2 000 in photovoltaics, nearly 2 000 in wind power and 1 000 in solar thermal, in comparison to approximately 600 jobs in 2013, principally in solar water heaters (IRENA, 2021[17]).

The need for effective public private partnerships for infrastructure in climate and energy related sectors has been exacerbated by growing energy supply and resource needs caused by the pandemic.

Climate change impacts infrastructure sectors in several domains including the water, transport, energy, ICT, urban development and solid waste sectors. Damages caused by climate hazards due to inappropriate planning and design, poor construction, maintenance or mismanagement, specifically where considerations of climate change have not been considered can have devastating and costly effects, particularly for developing countries (Global Center on Adaptation, 2021[21]). With increased demand for energy supplies and weak or outdated infrastructure that is susceptible to increasingly extreme weather patterns, chronic stresses and acute shocks to infrastructure impact the MENA region especially harshly.

COVID-19 exacerbated the challenges facing MENA infrastructure with growth and macroeconomic volatility, declines in demand, supply disruptions, added health and safety regulations and the need for a change in operations and government policy or sector decisions to implement stimulus or social safety nets. New PPPs can help UfM countries in need to mobilise private sector finance required to enhance the resilience of infrastructure systems to the impacts of climate change (World Bank, 2021[22]).

PPPs in energy solutions and climate action can have an amplified impact for developing countries, especially MENA countries that are plagued with underlying effects of poor water, environment, climate and energy management. For example, investment to reduce air pollution by transitioning towards renewable energy, sanitation and waste management infrastructure generates savings in healthcare expenditure. Meanwhile, improved drainage and climate-resilient road infrastructure have proven to generate savings in maintenance costs, while reducing disruptions in infrastructure service (Bassi, Pallaske and Guzzetti, 2020[23]).

COVID-19 has also compelled countries to revise existing PPP agreements and their functioning, and this affects energy PPP in the same way as other PPP agreements. The pandemic highlighted the need for increasing coordination and cooperation for PPP and implementing more fluid forms of partnerships given the extreme complexity, uncertainty and high projected costs of preparing for and responding to the impacts of the pandemic and climate change (Harvard Zofnass Program, 2020[24]). Enforced communication among partners has to remain key to mitigate information asymmetry challenges for governments due to COVID-19.

Policy considerations

Key progressive aspects are still missing from policy landscapes in MENA countries, hindering investor support and confidence. Given that energy demand will continue to grow at exponential rates, while private sector interest in the sector is not increasing correspondingly (EIB, 2016[25]), addressing these policy deficiencies will be crucial for promoting the renewable energy sector to foreign and domestic investors. To aid the UfMs approach on encouraging a Mediterranean agenda for energy and climate action linked to the global agenda, as noted by the SEMed Private Renewable Energy Framework (UfM, 2021[13])and supporting reports on climate financing, this OECD report suggests that MENA countries support reinforce and adapt climate related policies in the following ways:

- *Support a systematic and comprehensive assessment of potential climate impacts on energy systems.* There is no one-size-fits-all solution to enhance the resilience of North African energy systems, because of the wide range of patterns and magnitude of potential climate impacts in the region. Instead, tailored policy measures based on systematic assessments of climate risks and impacts will help North African countries increase the resilience of their energy systems. The assessment should be based on scientific methodologies and established guidelines. Governments can provide technical support by commissioning research and making quality data and information available. Governments can also develop, support and implement capacity-building activities for the assessment. In addition to the support for the science-policy nexus covered by the UfM Climate Action Plan (UfM, 2019), this report suggests that furthering opportunities for research on green recovery tools in the wake of the pandemic can be a strong tool to improve evaluations and encourage the inclusion of youth and research institutions in climate action policymaking. Not only will expanding such opportunities allow for further detailed assessments on how COVID-19 affected the implementation of the action plan, for example, in relation to nationally determined contribution implementation or mapping of interconnected supply chains to ensure stable movement of goods and services in the future.
- *Avoid postponement of climate-related projects due to the prioritisation of immediate economic recovery.* This is counterproductive to long-term climate efforts. Moreover, energy related infrastructure projects are a good way to boost economic recovery, employment and improve future economic growth. MENA countries should expand efforts to promote climate and energy solution sectors as strong investment opportunities, in line with the UfM report on Tracking and Enhancing International Private Climate Finance in the SEMed Region (UfM, 2019[26])and drawing on experience and evidence included in the UfM report on Climate Finance Flows in the SEMed Region (Borde and Righi, 2020[27]). These economies should focus on green recovery efforts that take such investments and projects at the centre of economic stimulus packages, in principle, avoiding postponement of renewable energy related projects while providing solutions for economic recovery.
- *Enhance public private partnerships opportunities in renewable energy and update PPP frameworks to include climate specific incentives.* PPPs offer a unique opportunity to make the MENA region an active player for renewable solutions to increasing energy needs. However, PPP infrastructure in the region remains weak, hindering opportunities to attract investors. Complementing UfM's recommendations on PPP in the water sector (UfM, 2019[28]), which point to enhancing cross-institutional interaction and capacity development, this report calls for MENA countries to focus on improving stakeholder engagement and communication, integrating key tools and capacities on climate resilience into PPP, and embedding resilience into existing frameworks of PPP. A set of OECD tools, including the OECD Principles for Public Governance of Public-Private Partnerships (OECD, 2012[29]), the Public-Private Partnerships Reference Guide (OECD and World Bank, 2017[30]) and the OECD policy considerations on climate resilient infrastructure (OECD, n.d.[31]) provide useful guidance on building resilient PPP frameworks.
- *As prioritising climate action in the MENA region's economic recovery can prove challenging, small scale private action at the local levels can help bridge the gap.* Despite some heterogeneous actions such as plastic pollution, there are relatively few government strategies on climate change in the region compared to European Mediterranean countries. The region has to cope with its political limitations that result from a lack of social cohesion and instability. Put simply, when priorities are focused on ensuring electricity supply and distribution, spotlighting climate action can be challenging. Private actions at the local and municipal levels in urban setting, such as urban mobility shift from car to bike sharing initiatives in cities (as discussed in chapter 5), can often be the first step towards more structured government responses.

Protect biodiversity and natural resources

> *Despite less coastal traffic due to COVID-19, rising sea levels and coastal erosion are on track to devastate major MENA cities while biodiversity loss remains on the rise*

While 40% of the world's population live in coastal areas, the share of total population living in the vicinity of the coast in the Maghreb is even higher, ranging from 65% in Morocco to 85% in Tunisia (Maul & Duedall, 2019). As the region's 7 500 km of coasts are home to every countries' capitals as well as major cities, growing urban density is increasing the portion of the population that could be affected by coastal erosion.

Coastal infrastructure plays a large role in the region's global trade through ports and shipping transits, providing efficient trade routes between the African and European continents. Moreover, intact beaches and coasts directly affect livelihoods and major industries in the region, have important indirect effects on economic revenues for the tourism reliant countries and remain important determinants for how much hotels can charge and the willingness of tourists to return (Heger and Vashold, 2021[32]).

Coasts are disproportionately vital to Maghreb economies, so coastal erosion is a major concern. Global average coastline recession is about 0.07 meters per year (m/yr). However, Tunisia has a rate of coastline recession 10 times higher, reaching approximately 0.70 m/yr. Morocco's situation is also increasingly worrisome as the Atlantic coast is currently receding at a rate of 0.12 m/yr and its Mediterranean coast at 0.14 m/yr, twice the global average (Luijendijk et al., 2018[33]). Although coastal traffic in MENA countries has decreased due to a lack of tourism, movement protocols and businesses closures during the pandemic, there have been no reports of a slowdown in the rate of coastal erosion in the Maghreb region.

> *COVID-19 has not staved off biodiversity loss, which continues to rise at dangerous rates in the MENA countries*

The ecosystem degradation is driven by factors typically amplified in the broad MENA region. Land and sea-use change (particularly agricultural expansion), climate change, direct exploitation of wild species, invasive alien species, and pollution are all linked and shaped by indirect drivers, such as demographic and social changes like rapid urbanisation (as described in chapter 5) and lack of adequate climate and conservation related policies (as discussed in chapter 4). Unfortunately, biodiversity loss is a key driver of emerging infectious diseases, and poses a variety of other growing risks to businesses, society and the global economy (OECD, 2020[34]).

Although sources of coastal erosion are manifold, human-induced factors including coastal subsidence, coastal protections, tourism infrastructure or land reclamation heavily impact coastline changes. With coastal traffic severely decreased due to the pandemic, increased biodiversity and vegetation regrowth has the ability to contrast further erosion. For example, posidonia fields, vegetation native to the Mediterranean Sea, reduces the energy of waves and currents, stabilising the seabed and securing sediment which can protect against coastal erosion (Jeffries and Campogianni, 2021[35]). However, around 70% of habitat loss of Posidonia oceanica is projected by 2050 with a potential for functional extinction by 2100, with no signs of slowdown with the pandemic.

Policy considerations

- *Promote regional coordination for sustainable biodiversity and conservation efforts.* The UfM Regional Analysis on Nationally Determined Contributions underlines the need for identifying relevant synergies among UfM member countries in the South and East of the Mediterranean (UfM, 2020[5]). The report stresses the dependence of the region's protected area management on connectivity and interconnected areas that state-levels cannot reach alone. Complementing the principles laid out in the UfM analysis, this OECD report recommends increasing the comprehensiveness and alignment of national policies before tackling regional programmes.

Coherence among national strategies and plans for environmental well-being should be ensured to streamline efforts, as adherence to multilateral mechanisms and agreements on environment is lacking. Horizontal and vertical institutional coordination on a local and national level is key for policy alignment in the nexus between land-use, biodiversity, climate, water and food and can help avoid overlapping or contradictory policy objectives, which will help streamline regional efforts in the long-run. The OECD's recent guidance on sustainable land use by aligning biodiversity, climate and food policies (OECD, 2020[36]) can be a useful tool in achieving these objectives.

Reduce Pollution

COVID-19 recovery in MENA countries should prioritise quickly implementable projects for greening the economy, and pollution mitigation programmes offer a good starting point

As noted in chapter 5, the broad MENA region faces serious pollution challenges, with the highest air pollution levels after South Asia, making climate change a growing long-term concern. While the impact of COVID-19 on water and air pollution has been discussed in Chapters 4 and 5 of the report, projects and guidelines to implement pollution mitigation programmes can be further elaborated upon. Quickly implementable infrastructure projects provide potential for fast and strong economic recovery by opening employment opportunities for many people (Hallegatte and Hammer, 2020[37]). Infrastructure projects in pollution abatement sectors such as fuel switching, energy efficiency and end-of-pipe projects are shovel ready and can spearhead a rapid but sustainable economic recovery, making them COVID-19 relevant. Pollution mitigation projects, especially for a region harshly impacted by deteriorating air quality as industries start to pick up in the wake of the pandemic, offer a chance to integrate green solutions into economic recovery from COVID-19 impacts.

There are strong pollution mitigation projects in MENA countries that offer solid opportunities to scale up private action in the fight against climate change.

- In **Lebanon**, the Lebanese Environmental Pollution Abatement Project (LEPAP) offered to firms in heavy polluting industries credit at near 0% interest rates for a period of 7 years. LEPAP has provided this concessional funding to fuel switching, energy efficiency and end-of-pipe projects (Ministry of Economy of Lebanon, 2021[38]).
- In **Jordan**, the Green Growth National Action Plan 2021-2025, approved in 2020, promotes green growth, climate change action and sustainable development through sectoral planning in the agriculture, energy, tourism, transport, waste and management sectors. The Plan aims to reduce fuel use and import dependence to ensure sustainable economic growth while decreasing unemployment and poverty (Ministry of Environment of Jordan, 2020[39]).
- In **Egypt**, the Environmental Pollution Abatement Project (EPAP) project helped industry improve performance and comply with environmental regulations. Eligible industries in Greater Cairo and Alexandria could borrow funds for fuel switching, energy efficiency, and end-of-pipe technologies at near zero interest rates. The project's second phase ended in 2016, allowing for initial replicability for neighboring countries. Phase 3 implementation is ongoing until 2022 (Ministry of Environment of Egypt, 2017[40]). The Air and Climate Pollution Reduction Project, funded by the World Bank, aims to reduce pollution from the transport sector and the solid waste management sector, which are the two largest contributors to emissions in the Greater Cairo area (World Bank, 2020[41]).

Policy considerations

Pollution reduction efforts continue to be hindered by inefficient policies and incentives that do not properly reward low carbon output goals. Encouraging citizens, particularly at the household level, to use energy efficient solutions will be an effective way to grow national awareness and support for the use of small-scale action to prevent climate change.

- *Align cross-sectoral policies to lower carbon output.* Efforts to stimulate economic recovery in the wake of COVID-19 offer an opportunity to align incentivising factors for energy efficiency and implement new climate mandates across several sectors. Such policies are typically found in mandates for energy efficiency targets, energy efficiency standards for firms, fuel efficiency standards for vehicles, fuel switching, end-of-pipe technologies and pricing pollution/carbon, and removing harmful subsidies that contribute to pollution and carbon use. For the broad MENA region in particular, **local level requirements in the form of energy efficiency standards for buildings, and minimum performance standards for appliances, such as air conditioners and refrigerators, hold high promise**. Using the UfM SEMed Private Renewable Energy Framework as a guideline, MENA countries may consider following the suggestions laid out by the OECD on aligning policies for low carbon economies (OECD, 2015[42]).

References

Bassi, A., G. Pallaske and M. Guzzetti (2020), *Post-COVID19 Recovery: Harnessing the Power of Investment in Sustainable Infrastructure*, https://www.orfonline.org/research/post-covid19-recovery/. [23]

Bianchi, M. (2020), *Prospects for Energy Transition in the Mediterranean after COVID-19*, https://www.iai.it/sites/default/files/iaip2018.pdf. [10]

Borde, A. and T. Righi (2020), *Climate Finance Flows in the SEMed Region in 2018*, https://ufmsecretariat.org/wp-content/uploads/2021/01/Climate-Finance-Flows-in-SEMed-Region-2018.pdf. [27]

Dabrowski, M. and M. Dominguez-Jimenez (2021), *The socio-economic consequences of COVID-19 in the Middle East and North Africa*, https://www.bruegel.org/2021/06/the-socio-economic-consequences-of-covid-19-in-the-middle-east-and-north-africa/. [7]

EIB (2016), *What's Holding back the Private Sector in MENA? Lessons learned from the enterprise survey.*, https://www.eib.org/attachments/efs/econ_mena_enterprise_survey_en.pdf. [25]

Energy and Climate Intelligence Unit (2021), *Net Zero Scorecard*, https://eciu.net/netzerotracker. [6]

Global Center on Adaptation (2021), *Climate-Resilient Infrastructure Officer Handbook: Knowledge Module on Public-Private Partnerships for Climate-Resilient Infrastructure*, https://gca.org/reports/climate-resilient-infrastructure-officer-handbook/. [21]

Global Data (2021), *Middle East renewables surge as energy transition accelerates*, https://power.nridigital.com/future_power_technology_sep21/middle_east_renewables. [16]

Hallegatte, S. and S. Hammer (2020), *Thinking ahead: For a sustainable recovery from COVID-19 (Coronavirus)*, https://blogs.worldbank.org/climatechange/thinking-ahead-sustainable-recovery-covid-19-coronavirus?deliveryName=DM65761. [37]

Harvard Zofnass Program (2020), *A Lesson from COVID-19: Re-envisioning Public Private Partnerships*, https://research.gsd.harvard.edu/zofnass/menu/events/forthcoming/re-envisioning-public-private-partnerships/. [24]

Heger, M. and L. Vashold (2021), *Disappearing coasts in the Maghreb: Coastal Erosion and its Costs*, https://thedocs.worldbank.org/en/doc/8320c30ab5eee11e7ec39f7f9496b936-0280012021/original/Note-Cost-of-Coastal-Erosion-En.pdf. [32]

Hussein, B. (2020), *Energy sector diversification: Meeting demographic challenges in the MENA region*, https://www.atlanticcouncil.org/in-depth-research-reports/report/energy-sector-diversification-meeting-demographic-challenges-in-the-mena-region/. [9]

IEA (2020), *The Oil and Gas Industry in Energy Transitions*, https://www.iea.org/reports/the-oil-and-gas-industry-in-energy-transitions. [8]

ILO (2021), *Renewable energy jobs have reached 12 million globally*, https://www.ilo.org/global/about-the-ilo/newsroom/news/WCMS_823759/lang--en/index.htm. [18]

IRENA (2021), *Renewable Capacity Statistics*, https://www.irena.org/-/media/Files/IRENA/Agency/Publication/2021/Apr/IRENA_RE_Capacity_Statistics_2021.pdf. [14]

IRENA (2021), *Renewable Energy and Jobs*, https://en.econostrum.info/attachment/2221736/. [17]

IRENA (2020), *MENA Country Specific Renewables Readiness Assessments*, https://www.irena.org/mena. [2]

IRENA (2020), *Renewable Energy Employment by Country*, https://www.irena.org/Statistics/View-Data-by-Topic/Benefits/Renewable-Energy-Employment-by-Country. [19]

Jeffries, E. and S. Campogianni (2021), *The Climate Change Effect in the Mediterranean: Six stories from an overheating sea*, https://www.wwf.fr/sites/default/files/doc-2021-06/20210607_Rapport_The-Climate-Change-Effect-In-The-Mediterranean-Six-stories-from-an-overheating-sea_WWF-min.pdf. [35]

Le Matin Maroc (2021), *Énergies renouvelables dans le mix électrique : Le Maroc relève à 64,3% ses ambitions pour 2030*, https://lematin.ma/journal/2021/energies-renouvelables-mix-electrique-maroc-releve-643-ambitions-2030/366328.html. [1]

Luijendijk, A. et al. (2018), "The State of the World's Beaches", *Scientific Reports*, https://doi.org/10.1038/s41598-018-24630-6. [33]

Ministry of Economy of Lebanon (2021), *Lebanon Environmental Pollution Abatement Project*, https://lepap.moe.gov.lb/?q=content/about-us. [38]

Ministry of Energy and Mineral Resources of Jordan (2020), *National Energy Sector Strategy 2020-2030*, https://www.memr.gov.jo/AR/Pages/%D8%A7%D8%B3%D8%AA%D8%B1%D8%A7%D8%AA%D9%8A%D8%AC%D9%8A%D8%A9_%D9%82%D8%B7%D8%A7%D8%B9_%D8%A7%D9%84%D8%B7%D8%A7%D9%82%D8%A9. [3]

Ministry of Environment of Egypt (2017), *Egypt Pollution Abatement Project III*, https://www.eeaa.gov.eg/portals/0/eeaaReports/N-EPAP/EPAP%20III/EPAP%20III%20Arabic%20updated.pdf. [40]

Ministry of Environment of Jordan (2020), *Green Growth National Action Plan 2021-2025*, https://www.edama.jo/wp-content/uploads/2021/08/Green-Growth-National-Action-Plan-2021-2025.pdf. [39]

OECD (2021), *Regional Integration in the Union for the Mediterranean: Progress Report*, https://www.oecd.org/science/regional-integration-in-the-union-for-the-mediterranean-325884b3-en.htm. [11]

OECD (2020), *Biodiversity and the economic response to COVID-19: Ensuring a green and resilient recovery*, https://www.oecd.org/coronavirus/policy-responses/biodiversity-and-the-economic-response-to-covid-19-ensuring-a-green-and-resilient-recovery-d98b5a09/. [34]

OECD (2020), *Towards Sustainable Land Use: Aligning Biodiversity, Climate and Food Policies*, OECD Publishing, Paris, https://doi.org/10.1787/3809b6a1-en. [36]

OECD (2015), *Aligning Policies for Low Carbon Economies*, https://www.oecd.org/environment/Aligning-Policies-for-a-Low-carbon-Economy.pdf. [42]

OECD (2014), *Public-Private Partnerships in the Middle East and North Africa*, https://www.oecd.org/mena/competitiveness/PPP%20Handbook_EN_with_covers.pdf. [15]

OECD (2012), *Recommendation of the Council on Principles for Public Governance of Public-Private Partnerships*, https://www.oecd.org/gov/budgeting/oecd-principles-for-public-governance-of-public-private-partnerships.htm. [29]

OECD (n.d.), *OECD Environment Policy Papers*, OECD Publishing, Paris, https://doi.org/10.1787/23097841. [31]

OECD and World Bank (2017), *Public-Private Partnerships Reference Guide - Version 3*, https://www.oecd.org/gov/world-bank-public-private-partnerships-reference-guide-version-3.htm. [30]

RCREEE and GWS (2010), *Country Report Jordan*, https://rcreee.org/content/country-report-jordan. [20]

UfM (2021), *SEMed Private Renewable Energy Framework “SPREF”*, https://ufmsecretariat.org/wp-content/uploads/2021/07/Leaflet_CA_03_APRIL2021-08_digital.pdf. [13]

UfM (2020), *Regional Analysis on Nationally Determined Contributions (NDCs) - 2nd Phase*, https://ufmsecretariat.org/wp-content/uploads/2021/01/Enhancement-of-NDCs-in-the-SEMed-Region_WEB.pdf. [5]

UfM (2019), *Public-Private Partnerships and the Financial Sustainability of the Mediterranean Water Sector*, https://ufmsecretariat.org/wp-content/uploads/2021/06/UfM-Water-Investment-Report.pdf. [28]

UfM (2019), *Tracking and enhancing international private climate finance in the Southern-Mediterranean Region*, https://ufmsecretariat.org/wp-content/uploads/2019/09/Private-Climate-Finance-Tracking-and-enhancing-international-private-climate-finance-in-the-Southern-Mediterranean-Region.pdf. [26]

UNEP/MAP and Plan Bleu (2020), *State of the Environment and Development in the Mediterranean*, https://planbleu.org/wp-content/uploads/2021/04/SoED_full-report.pdf. [4]

World Bank (2021), *COVID-19 and Public-Private Partnerships Practice Note*, https://library.pppknowledgelab.org/documents/6027. [22]

World Bank (2020), *New Project to Support the Improvement of Air Quality and the Fight Against Climate Change in Greater Cairo*, https://www.worldbank.org/en/news/press-release/2020/09/30/new-project-to-support-the-improvement-of-air-quality-and-the-fight-against-climate-change-in-greater-cairo. [41]

World Bank (2018), *World Development Indicators*, https://data.worldbank.org/indicator/EG.FEC.RNEW.ZS. [12]

Notes

[1] In this chapter, MENA region or MENA countries refer to the group of countries that are members of the Union for the Mediterranean. These countries are: Algeria, Egypt, Jordan, Lebanon, Mauritania, Morocco, Palestinian Authority and Tunisia. Where the term "broad MENA region" is used, it refers to the group of MENA countries that include UfM and non UfM members.

www.ingramcontent.com/pod-product-compliance
Lightning Source LLC
LaVergne TN
LVHW081410110826
845149LV00010B/1689

* 9 7 8 9 2 6 4 5 8 9 7 5 9 *